Trust in the Balance

Trust in the Balance

Building Successful Organizations on Results, Integrity, and Concern

Robert Bruce Shaw

JOSSEY-BASS
A Wiley Imprint
www.josseybass.com

Published by Jossey-Bass
A Wiley Imprint
989 Market Street, San Francisco, CA 94103-1741   www.josseybass.com

Jossey-Bass books and products are available through most bookstores. To contact
Jossey-Bass directly call our Customer Care Department within the U.S. at 800-956-7739,
outside the U.S. at 317-572-3986 or fax 317-572-4002.

Jossey-Bass also publishes its books in a variety of electronic formats. Some content that
appears in print may not be available in electronic books.

Library of Congress Cataloging-in-Publication Data

Shaw, Robert B., date.
    Trust in the balance : building successful organizations on results, integrity,
and concern / Robert Bruce Shaw.
      p. cm. — (The Jossey-Bass business & management series)
      Includes bibliographical references and index.
      ISBN 0–7879–0286–1 (alk. paper)
      1. Organizational behavior. 2. Trust (Psychology) I. Title. II. Series.
  HD58.7.S48 1997
      658.3'14—dc21
96–52978

FIRST EDITION
HB Printing 10 9 8 7 6 5

The Jossey-Bass
Business & Management Series

Contents

Trust-Building Resources

Preface

Above all, success in business requires two things: a winning competitive strategy and superb organizational execution. Distrust is the enemy of both. Many of the failures we see in business today result from suspicion among those who must think and act collaboratively in order for a business to thrive. As a management consultant, I have found that divergent strategic goals and unclear performance targets are often caused by mistrust. Distrust also results in poorly designed and implemented change initiatives. In other words, distrust is the source of many of the problems that plague our organizations.

Most of us have seen executive groups torn apart by pervasive suspicion. Leaders who distrust each other have trouble resolving their differences and rarely unite behind a clear vision for their firm. Nor can they effectively implement large-scale initiatives, because these inevitably require shared understanding and mutual support.

But the impact of distrust reaches far beyond the executive boardroom. Distrust can permeate an organization and undermine its ability to adapt to a changing competitive environment. Anyone who has worked in a large organization understands the tendency of different groups to distrust one another. In many firms, functional, product, and regional groups work in self-serving, if not outright antagonistic, ways.

In the new competitive economy, distrust has become much more than a human resource issue. Organizations with high levels of distrust are actually at a competitive disadvantage. In contrast, organizations that build on a foundation of trust are best positioned to achieve predictable business outcomes under rapidly changing and stressful conditions. Trust, from this perspective, is one of the most important factors in achieving "hard" business results.

This book is about building communities of trust within business settings. It explores the changes that are making trust essential and presents a new approach to creating and sustaining trust in the face of adversity.

Trust Is Vital for Business Success

The importance of trust becomes clear when we try to imagine a world without it. In such a world, each of us would live in a state of chronic suspicion. At best, people would be indifferent to others. At worst, they would be fearful of each other. In a world without trust, leaders are seen as self-serving and manipulative. Few people are willing to follow them. No one feels confident about others' abilities—only the foolhardy or desperate seek advice or support. In such a world, people prefer to work alone or in small family-like groups. They are afraid of depending on people they didn't know. A commitment to a project or goal becomes meaningless since it might, or might not, be fulfilled. All transactions take place in cash as people do not trust that they will receive payment for products delivered or services rendered. People assume that public pronouncements are designed to mislead. In such a world, to be leery of others is the only pragmatic attitude to take. In a world without trust, lawyers are in great demand.

While some of these characteristics are all too familiar, a world completely devoid of trust can exist only in our imagination. We cannot survive without others. Thus, we trust because we have no choice but to depend on other people. How many of us can produce our own food and water? Cure ourselves when we are sick? Build a protective shelter? In each case, we must rely on the goodwill and ability of others if we are to survive. Similarly, in business, what can be done without mutual interdependence? Show me the employee who does not depend on the support of others to accomplish his or her job. Describe the business that is not built on a myriad of often subtle agreements and obligations that transcend any legal stipulations. Identify the firm that does not depend on suppliers to meet their cost and quality commitments. Name the leader who does not base his or her actions on information that others within the organization provide. In short, we have no choice but to deal with the dilemmas of trust, for trust is at the core of all business activity; virtually all economic activity is carried out by groups of people who depend on each other.

Most perspectives on trust focus too narrowly on the personality or character of those we trust and those we don't. But to influence business outcomes significantly, trust must be treated as a structural and cultural characteristic of organizations. Trust, from this point of view, influences performance on four different levels:

- *Organizational success:* The performance of a firm requires trust in order to empower individuals, teams, and groups to act on a wide range of strategic objectives.
- *Team effectiveness:* Teams depend on the ability of people to work interdependently in order to realize a common goal. Superior team performance is rarely found without high levels of trust.
- *One-on-one collaboration:* Working directly with others requires that we trust one another enough to share information, unite behind objectives, take necessary risks, and deal effectively with adversity.
- *Individual credibility:* The degree to which people are given the autonomy, resources, and support needed to perform their jobs requires that others trust them. This is true for all organizational members but particularly important for those in leadership positions. People are more likely to support those whom they believe to be trustworthy.

Trust Is Becoming More Elusive

While trust is becoming more important to business success, it is also becoming more difficult to achieve as firms change the way they operate. Shareowner advocacy and competitive pressures have dramatically increased the demand for bottom-line results, and this often leads to ongoing cost cutting and restructuring. Major reorganizations have resulted in widespread changes in employees' job responsibilities and reporting relationships. Many employees feel that the new work environment requires more of them while providing less job security and stability in return. The changes we are undergoing are described by some as a break in the "psychological contract" that existed between a company and its members. In the past, employees of most large firms believed that the company would provide a reasonable salary and long-term job security in return for a fair day's work. In the new environment, corporations are more likely to question the function—and in many cases, the necessity—of almost every job. Thousands of people are being removed from the corporate payrolls, and many of those who remain are placed in new roles. These gut-wrenching changes are occurring at the same time that profits and executive compensation have reached record levels. It is not surprising that in many firms, trust is in short supply.

The erosion of trust, however, is more than a response to the downsizings and restructurings of the past decade. We are seeing the emergence of a new type of organization that undermines the familiarity needed to sustain trust. New information technologies are resulting in what some call a "virtual organization," where personal contact among employees is transitory or even nonexistent. People are being asked to trust others whom they know little or not at all. They are being asked to make themselves more vulnerable to others than ever before. Consider, for example, the use of rewards that link an individual's pay to the performance of people whom he or she sees infrequently and knows only indirectly.

In short, we face a basic dilemma: dramatic economic and business changes are making trust both more important and more elusive. Trust is necessary in the new marketplace. You can't compete without it. Yet the competitive environment that makes trust more important is also making it more difficult to sustain. What was hard is getting harder. How do you build trust in today's competitive business environment?

Trust requires more than a softhearted approach to human relations. Trust requires more than creating a supportive environment. It requires a tough set of actions and procedures that may even appear ruthless or coldhearted to some people. For example, trust in a business setting requires, in part, that we feel confident that others will deliver on their commitments. Trust is impossible when a large percentage of a firm's employees cannot meet their business commitments. Building a trust-based organization requires that firms move or remove those who fail to perform despite sufficient feedback and coaching. This is necessary even if those impacted are wonderful, hardworking people with the best of intentions. Similarly, building a trust-based organization requires that those who violate principles of integrity be removed immediately in order to reinforce the importance of conducting business by a set of accepted practices. Otherwise, the viability of the entire enterprise is at risk. Few organizations, however, have the capacity or conviction required to make these difficult decisions.

Building trust requires attention to every aspect of a firm's design—its structure, management policies and practices, technological systems, informal culture, the values and expectations of its members, and the behavior of those in leadership positions. This book is about creating organizations that sustain trust in the face of the economic and competitive pressures that make distrust more likely—and more troublesome.

Who Will Benefit from This Book?

This book offers pragmatic advice to those who seek to build trust-based organizations and teams. In particular, I focus on the challenges facing the senior leaders of large corporations, as well as those leading divisions or large business groups. I answer a few basic questions that are especially important to those in leadership positions:

- What is trust? What does a high-trust organization or group look like? How can we assess the level of trust in an organization or group?
- Why is trust important in high-performance organizations and groups? How is trust related to bottom-line results?
- What are the key factors that promote trust in an organization or group? What produces distrust?
- Why is trust so hard to win and so easy to lose? Can an organization or group regain trust once it has been lost?
- What can a leader do to build a high-trust organization or group?
- What is the best way to deal with chronic levels of distrust?

Although this book is written for those seeking to build high-trust organizations and groups, it is not a "how-to" manual that offers easy answers. Building trust requires that each leader and his or her organization struggle with the dilemmas inherent in establishing and maintaining trust. My goal is to outline these dilemmas and suggest possible actions based on a set of guiding principles. These suggested actions are illustrated with examples taken from firms that have mastered some or all of trust's dilemmas.

Building trust requires that we understand the need for both hard and soft approaches. While trust requires some tough actions on the part of every leader, I am certainly not advocating a retreat to traditional, hierarchical, "command and control" management. Nor I am suggesting that leaders focus only on the bottom line, doing whatever is required to deliver financial results. Instead, this book reflects my belief that one-sided "New Age" approaches, which deal only with the soft side of trust, will not work over the long term because they deny the fundamental challenges facing any large business. Trust is a dilemma because it requires actions that at times conflict with one another. The role of the leader is to recognize and, to the best of his or her ability, manage these tradeoffs.

How to Use the Book to Build Trust

Trust in the Balance is organized into four parts. In Part One, I define trust and present the imperatives on which it is built. In Chapter One, I describe the business forces that are making trust ever more important *and* more elusive. In Chapter Two, I outline a research-based model to help explain why trust develops in some organizations and teams and not in others.

In Part Two, I elaborate on the model of organizational trust presented in the second chapter. In Chapters Three, Four, and Five, I describe each of the key imperatives for building trust: achieving results, acting with integrity, and demonstrating concern. These chapters include extensive examples drawn from such firms as Pepsi, Hewlett-Packard, and GE. Assessment surveys at the end of Chapters Two through Five help readers measure how well they and their organizations are performing. This knowledge, along with the information provided throughout the book, will equip the reader to take actions that will increase trust.

In Part Three, I describe the key focal points within an organization for building trust. Chapter Six looks at the role of leadership in the development of a high-trust organization or team. In particular, I focus on the need for the leader to behave in a way that fosters trust and to serve as the key architect of organizational structures and processes that foster trust. Chapters Seven and Eight examine how the architecture and culture of an organization can be designed to sustain appropriate levels of trust that will lead to improved performance.

In the first chapter of Part Four, I examine specific trust dilemmas, such as those that arise during downsizing and reengineering efforts. In Chapter Ten, I present effective approaches for overcoming the challenges and obstacles inherent in situations of extreme distrust. Chapter Eleven addresses the problems of sustaining trust in the face of uncertainty and competing demands.

Sources of Support

My interest in trust began in the 1980s during a discussion with Dennis N. T. Perkins on the issues that would become increasingly important in determining the success of organizations. Dennis, who was then teaching at Yale, set me to thinking more about trust as a key element in business success. David Berg, who has written extensively on team dynamics, shared my interest in the topic and pushed me to look at trust from an organizational and group perspective (rather than an individual one). In my work over the past five years with Dick Beckhard, author and management consultant, the topic has never been far from the surface. His approach to organizational consulting embodies many of the trust imperatives I describe in this book. Finally, Joel Deluca,who teaches organizational behavior at Wharton, has provided fresh insights and ongoing support.

This book also draws on three streams of work related to trust. The most important and immediate source is my consulting work, which focuses on the issues involved in large-scale change, especially organizational design and leadership. The lessons I've learned from over a decade of this work form the heart of this book. I am indebted to my clients, typically senior leaders in Fortune 100 organizations, for giving me the opportunity to work with them on improving the performance of their firms. This work has greatly enriched my understanding of the role that trust plays in organizational life.

The overall trust model I present in this book also draws on applied research that includes the detailed comparative analyses of high- and low-trust organizations that I conducted for my dissertation.[1] Recent work by other researchers has supported and, in some cases, expanded on my findings.[2]

The third stream of support consists of a handful of authors who have explored trust. Charles Handy[3] suggests that trust will become more troublesome—and more important—with the rise of new organizational designs. His work examines the soft side of organizational life in a way that hard-edged business people can appreciate and use. Francis Fukuyama[4] has analyzed the relationship between the level of trust within a culture and its economic prosperity. His work contains a number of elegant insights into trust that I have used in this book. The sociologist Bernard Barber[5], an early advocate for balance in our view of trust (noting the need for alternative control mechanisms to ensure that appropriate levels of trust are sustained), also influenced my views on trust. Finally, Niklas Luhman[6] reinforced the central role of trust in everyday life and the importance of viewing trust from an organizational and societal point of view.

I am also grateful to the many skilled professionals at Jossey-Bass. Cedric Crocker, as the managing editor, supported the book's development in a variety of ways and is one of the primary reasons I enjoy working with Jossey-Bass. Terri Welch contributed ideas about positioning the book and convinced me of the need to build the work around a few central themes. Janet Hunter, as editor, provided wonderful input and helped improve the book's overall organization and flow. The Jossey-Bass community, in total, embodies many of the attributes described in this book.

Princeton, New Jersey   ROBERT BRUCE SHAW
January 1997

The Author

Robert Bruce Shaw assists business leaders in building organizations capable of superior performance in rapidly changing industries. He provides advice on the development and implementation of new competitive strategies aimed at increasing long-term profitability and growth. Such work often requires an integrated and disciplined approach to transforming a firm's structure, culture, work systems, and people. Shaw's clients, senior leaders in Fortune 500 firms, span a wide variety of industries including financial services, telecommunications, industrial products, pharmaceuticals, and consumer goods.

Shaw is the founder of Princeton MCG. He holds a Ph.D. in organizational behavior from Yale University and has authored or coauthored a number of books and articles on organizational performance, including *Discontinuous Change: Leading Organizational Transformation* and *Organizational Architecture: Designs for Changing Organizations.* He is a frequent speaker on the topics of organizational architecture, leadership, and change.

Trust in the Balance

Trust
A Foundation for Organizational Success

Part One introduces trust as a central component of organizational success. My approach to trust contrasts with a psychological perspective (which holds that trust is primarily an issue between individuals). From a broader point of view, trust is a powerful force that influences what occurs both within and between organizations.

In the two chapters of this section, I highlight several key themes:

1. Trust is becoming more important as organizations struggle to gain advantage in highly competitive markets. In particular, trust is an absolute necessity when organizations depend on "coordinated empowerment," which gives people the autonomy they need to perform yet requires that they actively collaborate to realize company objectives.

2. Trust is becoming more elusive as organizations strive to increase their profitability. In the process, many are dramatically cutting costs and reengineering the way they operate. Many have broken the "security contract" that existed between organizations and their employees for most of this century.

3. Trust is governed by rules that make it extremely difficult to regain once lost. Therefore, trust is best treated as an asset that leaders must protect and, as needed, leverage (just as they do with other corporate resources).

In sum, Chapters One and Two provide a new way of thinking about the importance of trust and a set of basic concepts that will be used throughout the book.

Chapter One

The Power of Trust in a Changing World

The reality of today's business environment is clear: embrace change or die. Competitive advantage arises not from a firm's historical strengths but from its ability to build new strengths in relation to emerging threats and opportunities. In other words, competitive advantage comes from an organization's ability to use its current resources to replace what worked in the past with new and innovative approaches. Building new strengths requires that firms abandon, at least in part, past practices.

Consider, for example, the recent shift in Microsoft's strategy. One of the fastest-growing and most successful firms in history, Microsoft dominated a world of highly decentralized computing. But the emergence of the Internet, making possible a world of truly shared computing, has challenged Microsoft's fundamental approach. Microsoft has recently altered its business strategy and is realigning its organization to address the opportunities presented by this new world of Internet computing. The next few years will tell whether Microsoft can effectively execute its new strategy and achieve the success it has enjoyed over the past decade. Ironically, the challenge Microsoft is facing now is similar in scope to the one IBM faced in moving beyond a world of mainframe computing. This challenge is to leverage the strengths that accounted for Microsoft's success in the past.

Trust among organizational members increases the likelihood of successful change. That is, trust increases the likelihood that people will abandon past practices in favor of new approaches. Trust is a resource, a form of "collaborative capital" that can be used to great advantage.[1] Hewlett-Packard, for example, has undergone organizational changes that would be difficult to achieve in less trusting cultures. HP has transformed itself several times over the course of its history and is constantly realigning its business units to meet customer and market demands. While HP's values have remained constant, the organization has largely changed the customers it serves and the products it offers. Richard Simonds, an HP project manager, spoke about the important role of trust in managing the change process:

> At Hewlett-Packard, we have gone through a great deal of change in the move from being an instrument company to a computer company. I believe the level of trust within HP enables us to be extremely agile in reconfiguring how we operate. That is quite an advantage in relation to those firms that change only under great duress and, then, with only limited success.
>
> At Hewlett-Packard, the trust level is high enough that people believe they will not suffer as a result of a change. They are thus more likely to support new approaches. Here, people understand that we must evolve our structure and processes, embrace new ways of operating, in order to compete in the marketplace.

In contrast, firms with low levels of trust are fighting an uphill battle when they try to implement new operating principles and processes. They are at a competitive disadvantage because every step in the change process becomes more difficult and time consuming at all levels. They lack the collaborative capital needed to change the organization. Mutual trust is critical if employees are to support radical change, despite the stress and dislocation it may cause, and then move forward in building a new organization.

General Motors provides a notable example of how distrust can put an organization at a disadvantage. During the 1980s and early 1990s, GM went through numerous reorganizations. The goal was to improve dramatically the company's productivity and overall effectiveness in meeting customer needs. Yet despite its efforts to change, GM failed to keep pace with such competitors as Chrysler, Ford, and Toyota. These companies eroded GM's market share and developed superior product and manufacturing processes. In almost every key business area, GM was falling behind its increasingly strong competitors.[2]

GM's difficulties were the result of a wide range of strategic and organizational problems. Central to the firm's malaise, however, was the inability to articulate a clear strategic vision and then establish accountability deep within the organization. Many employees were suspicious of their leadership's vision for the future. To unite around a course of action, GM's employees had to believe that their management was capable of leading the company through difficult times. They also had to believe that all members of the firm would share in the necessary hardships and that employees would be compensated for their sacrifices if the firm's financial status improved. Management had to believe that employees cared about the health of the firm and would work to bring its costs in line with those of its competitors. In sum, all involved needed to work collaboratively to improve the firm's competitiveness.

The situation at GM revealed a lack of trust in both directions. Too many of GM's employees were angry with then CEO Roger Smith and actively resisted his change initiatives. Few employees believed that Smith had a strategy that would allow GM to build its market share; even fewer believed he cared about their well-being either as employees or as individuals. As a result, changes introduced by senior management at GM were either implemented poorly or not at all. GM's leadership, in turn, did not fully trust employees to act responsibly and, therefore, gave them less autonomy and power. The result was an organization in a quagmire. Smith became increasingly frustrated with the slow pace of change and looked to technology, rather than human collaboration, to answer the challenges facing his firm. This focus was misguided and ultimately failed despite an investment of billions of dollars. For all the changes Smith and his leadership team introduced, the lack of trust at GM persisted as a major obstacle to significant change.

The Trust Imperative

GM is not alone in its need for trust. Indeed, the central theme of this book is that trust will become increasingly important as organizations struggle to adapt to today's turbulent business environment. The challenges facing firms as they prepare for an uncertain future demand that they embrace flatter, more flexible organizational structures. Only then will they be able to compete in the face of new competitive pressures. We are seeing the emergence of new types of team and organizational structures that require a higher degree of autonomy *and* collaboration. Old forms of control are being replaced by innovative approaches that give people far greater power than at any time in the past. Our new organizational designs minimize "command and control" approaches to management. For example, front-desk clerks at Ritz-Carlton hotels now have the authority to delete up to $2,000 from a guest's bill if a mistake has been made or poor service provided. Satisfying customers immediately is of paramount importance to the firm. This level of service, however, requires a high degree of trust in its employees.[3]

Several trends, in total, are converging to make trust a key competitive issue for organizations. As illustrated in Figure 1.1, these trends demand organizational responses that emphasize more empowerment *and* more collaboration. The most important organizational responses include:

- Empowerment of individuals and teams
- Radically redesigned business processes
- Near total business-unit autonomy and power
- Active collaboration across teams and groups
- Emergence of global alliances among firms
- Enhanced organizational learning

These trends move us away from the rigid bureaucratic organizational structures that dominated the corporate landscape for most of this century. The strict policies and procedures that accompany bureaucracy institutionalize distrust. After all, bureaucracies are based on the assumption that people will abuse power if we entrust them with it. Trust is replaced by formal regulations that force people to behave in ways deemed appropriate by those in positions of authority. New competitive demands, however, make this type of control too restrictive and time consuming. Thus, we are seeing the creation of new forms of organization and management that require higher levels of trust.

Yet trust is no panacea. It is essential in many situations— but not sufficient by itself to ensure success. For example, trust

Figure 1.1. New Business Challenges Demanding Higher Levels of Trust.

Increasingly Competitive Global Market

Business Challenges

- Financial results (grow revenue, reduce costs, deliver bottom line . . .)
- Customer results (meet or exceed expectations, build loyalty . . .)
- Employee results (gain alignment, develop capabilities, build ownership . . .)

Organizational Responses

- Empowered individuals and teams
- Horizontal business processes
- Business-unit autonomy and power
- Cross-group collaboration
- Alliances and joint ventures
- Real-time organizational learning

Vital Role of Trust

Higher levels of trust required for new organizational approaches to work

is necessary if teams are to perform at their best. Without it, team members will not collaborate in a productive manner. But more than trust is needed for a team to be successful; factors such as having a clear charter and goals, sufficient member knowledge and skill, appropriate roles, effective operating procedures, and learning mechanisms are also important. Thus, we should consider trust a key enabler, a foundation of support, for high performance.

The following sections look at the emerging organization responses to the new business challenges and describe how trust plays a critical role in each.

Empowered Individuals and Teams

Faced with new competitive pressures, organizations are also giving individuals and teams more responsibility and authority. Effectiveness requires that all employees be able to make decisions and commit resources on behalf of others in a way that is not unduly restricted. Within certain limits, effectiveness depends on people having a "blank check" in order to move forward with a particular strategy or course of action. Trust enables people at all levels to operate with more latitude in doing what is required to win in the marketplace.

The trustworthiness of another is an important consideration in providing that person with the authority to make key business decisions. If, for example, the senior leader of an organization is viewed as being untrustworthy, employees will actively or passively resist what he or she is trying to accomplish. Thus, a leader's options are severely limited by excessive and ongoing distrust among employees. When employee confidence erodes, leaders must devote increasing energy to ensuring that people will follow their direction.

Employees also need the power to make immediate decisions within their areas of authority. As with senior leaders, those being given power to make decisions must be trusted to act in a way that supports the best interests of the organization and its customers over the long term. Without trust, senior leadership will intervene or seek to control areas in which they have limited knowledge or expertise. As with individuals, teams cannot act effectively unless trusted to the degree necessary to fulfill their responsibilities. Moreover, a culture of trust within each group is essential if it is to take full advantage of the benefits of teamwork.

Trust is based on the assumption that people are both able and willing to use their power to advance the common good of the organization. The process of granting and receiving trust often increases the likelihood that people, at all levels, will act in a trustworthy manner. In other words, *in most cases,* trusting others makes them more trustworthy. Those in positions of authority feel pressured to fulfill their obligations in order to sustain the confidence of those who are dependent on them. They know that the trust they need to be effective will be lost if they fail to meet the expectations of others.

Firms that move down the path of empowerment quickly realize that they need superb people at every organizational level. Empowerment, all told, cannot work unless people are fully willing and able to fulfill the demands placed on them. Yet, the most talented people will be in great demand and, in many cases, able to select among various firms seeking to hire them. When given a choice, they will choose *not* to work in a suspicious, distrusting environment. Thus, those organizations that create a high-trust culture will be better able to attract the talented people they need to make empowerment work.

Redesigned Business Processes

Over the past decade, most firms have reengineered their core business processes in order to lower costs while simultaneously enhancing the value of their products and services. These efforts are intended to improve radically the way work is done. In most cases, reengineering involves the innovative use of technology to produce new approaches to core work practices. In successful applications, organizations have dramatically enhanced their productivity and their ability to react to changes in their marketplace.

Advocates of reengineering admit that the majority of such efforts fail.[4] Most of these failures spring from the inability of leaders and their organizations to manage the extreme cultural changes that come with reengineered business processes. Thus, the failures of reengineering are not technical failures—they are human failures. Elegant redesigns often fail because people will not support them.

Those involved in the process of reengineering must be willing to alter sources of power and work together in a new and more uncertain environment. Yet reengineered processes, by design, cut across functional and geographic boundaries that are often characterized by distrust. Many of the failed reengineering efforts with which I am familiar have resulted from the inability, or unwillingness, of functional leaders to work collaboratively and to let go of their traditional approaches to running a business. They lack the trust needed to let go of their standard operating procedures and individual sources of power. They support the reengineering process until it makes them vulnerable to each other and to employees at lower levels in the organization.

More and more organizations are being structured around horizontal business processes that cut across traditional functional areas of responsibility. The changes required have an impact on almost every aspect of a business and force difficult, sometimes courageous, actions. Coordination across groups, or the complete redesign of an organization around core business processes, requires an extremely high level of trust. Without that trust, rivalries among organizational groups can undermine any attempt at radical redesign.

Business-Unit Autonomy and Power

Many corporations are moving toward what some call a "federal organization" in which local business units operate much as sovereign states do in a political federation.[5] These local units must retain enough power to compete effectively in rapidly changing markets, while the corporate center must retain enough power to chart a strategic direction for the entire enterprise. Given the tension that almost always exists between largely autonomous business units and the corporate center, sustaining an appropriate balance is an extremely difficult task. Trust is one of the linchpins that holds the various parts together and allows for differences to be managed in a timely and effective manner. An organization based on this model cannot operate successfully without trust.

In "federal" organizations, relatively autonomous business units focus on particular customer and product segments of the market. Each group functions as an independent business—yet the firm is more than a holding company because there is coordination among the different businesses. Members of the business units are expected to deliver on their "local" financial commitments *and* support corporate-wide initiatives that will help the company sustain a competitive advantage overall. This "loosely coupled, highly aligned" organizational model requires a great deal of trust between the firm's corporate staff and the heads of the various business units. Each group must believe that it can depend on the other and that they are all working toward the same overall goal, even though their shorter-term agendas may differ.

Cross-Group Collaboration

GE's Jack Welch often talks of a boundaryless organization free of the restrictive barriers that divide most companies. This trend is being driven by a variety of factors, including:

- Customer requirements ("Why can't you solve my problem? I don't care how you are organized.")
- Innovation ("Why can't our R&D people work with our marketing staff to develop successful new products?")
- Growth ("Why can't we cross-sell to our customers throughout our different businesses?")
- Cost reduction ("Why do we have redundant staff functions in every business unit?")

In many organizations, the level of trust among key groups is low. Different groups often have not only divergent objectives but also differing points of view on how the business should operate. People in production, for example, may believe that those in sales care only about this quarter's targets in sales volume; in turn, people in sales may believe that the production team has lost touch with the marketplace. Many factions can develop along group lines, and these can ultimately erode an organization's ability to compete. Rivalries among groups (whether between management and labor, headquarters and field, staff groups and operations, or among an organization's various teams) are at best a distraction and at worst a competitive liability. Delivery of superior products and services requires active collaboration across various groups; yet collaboration is difficult, if not impossible, in a culture of distrust.

People who cannot trust each other will end up cooperating only under a system of formal rules and regulations, which may have to be negotiated and enforced, sometimes by coercive means.[6] In the worst cases, *excessive* formalization of mutual obligations takes time and energy away from collaboration on the vital tasks required for a firm to be competitive in a rapidly changing marketplace. In short, without trust, true cross-group collaboration is rarely more than rhetoric.

One of my clients, for example, has established a formal process to link the activities of its R&D organization and the firm's commercial divisions. In many respects, the new system helps to clarify expectations around priorities and links specific outcomes to rewards. But the system must evolve to the point where the relationship between R&D and the divisions has gone beyond formal requirements; individuals in each group must come to see each other as partners in helping the business to grow. Only when this comes about can the system be considered a true success.

Global Alliances and Joint Ventures

Another organizational response to the new competitive pressures involves the use of alliances and joint ventures among firms. Many firms are recognizing that they need to form partnerships with other organizations to obtain advantages superior to anything they could develop independently. Some need these alliances in order to gain access quickly to new technology or markets. They recognize that their need to develop unique technologies and products, penetrate new markets, or cut costs through consolidation demands new partnerships. Consider, for example, the alliance between Ford and ABB to build a paint-finishing plant for 75 percent of the normal cost; an added benefit was that the plant was finished sooner than if either company had worked alone.[7]

The arrangements between companies are as varied as the companies themselves, with different degrees of connectedness among the firms. These relationships range from full mergers to loose alliances in the marketing of particular products or services. The nature of these relationships varies with the purpose of the alliance; a constant, however, is the need to create an appropriate level of trust among those involved. Firms that cannot develop this trust will, in most markets, find themselves at a disadvantage to those firms that can effectively combine their offerings in unique and flexible ways to meet customer needs.

Alliances are extremely difficult to accomplish. Failed joint ventures are numerous.[8] The planned alliance between U.S. West and Time Warner for creating interactive services has been stalled by a bitter legal fight. Prodigy, the on-line service of IBM and Sears Roebuck, suffered enormous losses and fell behind its rivals amid conflicts over direction. Kaleida Labs, the Apple-IBM joint venture, is now dead because of indecision over the strategic and financial goals of the enterprise.

One research team examining the effectiveness of strategic alliances found that establishing trust was one of the most critical challenges. As one alliance manager observed, managers must have "the right chemistry with their counterparts in the partner firm" in order for the alliance to go anywhere. That "right chemistry" is organizational trust: trust within a firm and trust between a firm and its partner. The alliance manager must create and preserve both.[9] A research team at the University of Virginia reached a similar conclusion and noted that "creating an environment of trust is critical and it requires enormous effort and careful attention."[10]

Firms seeking to form partnerships must deal with different histories, different competitive strategies, different values, different cultures, and different operating procedures. They must also deal with suspicion, which is often evident from the start, as managers from both sides worry about the impact of the alliance on their jobs and their careers. The more diverse the firms, the more the potential for conflict and the more problems the partnership will experience. Consider the difficulty of establishing trust among firms as different as Apple and IBM: each has unique operating procedures, different managerial styles, and inconsistent expectations regarding the emerging relationship. While a myriad of factors will have an impact on the success of any joint venture, trust among the key parties is always critical.

Organizational Learning

The most successful firms learn quickly both about changing customer needs and about their mistakes in meeting those needs. To be efficient in this way—that is, to be learning organizations—they must rely in large measure on trust. In particular, trust is necessary if people are to be open and candid about the things that have gone wrong—and accurate about what is going right.

A high level of trust allows people to say what is on their minds and not feel that it will come back to hurt them. A sufficient level of trust ensures that lines of communication are open and that no one is hiding information or wasting time trying to decide the political implications of his or her views. A team that is comfortable with direct and honest communication is more likely to consider various alternatives to the problems it faces. Open lines of communication also result in better and more timely decisions. In this way, trust allows leaders to use the talents of the people on the team to their full extent, producing superior outcomes on whatever the team is trying to accomplish.[11] In contrast, in a low-trust organization, mistakes are viewed as an embarrassment that must be hidden from public scrutiny. Unless people can trust that they will not be harmed, the "postmortem" sessions needed to extract valuable lessons from failures either do not occur or become shallow exercises with little long-term value.

A firm's ability to survive depends on its ability to adapt quickly and effectively to changes in its environment and within its own operations. The rapid pace of change in most industries today means that corporations will need increasingly accurate and timely information in making key decisions. In particular, firms need to develop mechanisms for quickly obtaining, analyzing, and reacting to information of various types and from various sources. Formal systems, such as information technology, will continue to be helpful, but the informal culture of an organization will become equally important in developing an information-rich organization.

Employees need up-to-date information regarding company performance, customer satisfaction, and competitive initiatives. A high-trust culture is needed if people are to share such information, particularly negative information, with each other. People must trust that the information they receive is accurate and representative of the best knowledge and thinking within their firm. This is especially true for information moving up the corporate hierarchy.

Distrust inhibits the sharing of negative or painful information. It often results in an unwillingness to communicate negative information for fear of the consequences. As one midlevel manager working within a large Fortune 500 corporation said:

> It is very difficult to give bad news in this organization. If you give bad news, you are perceived—no, you are told that you are not "on the team." Bad news is telling your supervisors that a project will not work or a product is not acceptable. You are not on the team if you say that. I enjoy working here and am forced to go along with things that I would rather not. I do it because I think the good outweighs the bad in terms of this as a place to work. But I have been told that I am not a team player more than once.

This manager voiced a common concern: many believe that sharing information, particularly painful information, with those outside one's own team is a risky endeavor. Yet clearly, filtering or editing information because of distrust ultimately undermines the ability of an organization to adapt.

Trust itself does not guarantee success, but pervasive distrust makes an open and candid discussion of key issues, which is critical for learning, highly unlikely. If it prevents us from discussing our own firm's liabilities and failures, it decreases the chances for success.

The Limits of Trust

Trust is not always possible. Indeed, a reflection, distrust is often based on hard-earned knowledge and experience and not simply on irrational fears. Individuals, groups, and corporations have different preferred outcomes on many issues. One would need to be either ignorant or deluded to have total, or blind, trust. Distrust allows us to be on guard against the potentially destructive motives and actions of others that could cause us significant harm.

Ironically, the increased need for trust in our new organizational designs makes the role of checks and balances even more important than in traditional firms. High-trust firms are more vulnerable because many of the rigid controls found in lower-trust firms have been removed. Violations of trust, which are more likely when controls are completely lacking, can result in a rise of chronic and debilitating distrust and, ultimately, in organizational failure. Some basic safeguards are needed in order to allow people to sustain their trust in an increasingly chaotic and fast-paced world.

Many believe that trust implies a complete absence of organizational controls. Some even find the word *control* at odds with the ideal of trust. While high-trust organizations usually have fewer and less rigid controls, they still have them. The reason is easily stated: some people and groups, although a small number, will act in ways that can harm an organization. We have seen, for example, firms that had insufficient controls. In the case of Barings Bank, a twenty-eight–year-old employee was allowed to engage in enormous and risky financial trades that ultimately cost his bank $1.3 billion in losses.[12] These losses consumed the investment bank's $900 million in capital and forced the 233-year-old institution into bankruptcy and eventual sale to pay off its debts. The trader's deals exposed the firm's entire capital base, risking far more than almost all the transactions in the firm's history put together. At the time, the new market of global trading in highly volatile securities offered huge profits to those corporations willing to allow aggressive traders free rein. Many firms ignored the need for safeguards and even provided incentives for traders to behave as aggressively as possible. Barings advanced over $500 million in the belief that the funds were being used as loans to clients for their trading activity—not once checking to determine if in fact this was the case. Instead, it appears that Barings' trader engaged in a complex and systematic process of deception and false accounting. Because the institution lacked the sufficient and appropriate controls, it was brought to its knees through the actions of a single individual, stunning both the organization and the entire business community.[13]

This example illustrates the risks of empowerment in a highly volatile industry. Whether Barings had a clear strategy for empowering its employees or could be considered to be a high-trust organization is not especially relevant. What its experience illustrates, beyond doubt, is that every organization needs some *small* number of effective safeguards to ensure that unethical behavior or high-impact mistakes are not capable of becoming fatal. Without safeguards, the vitality and integrity of an entire organization are at risk. The question, then, becomes how to build organizations with checks and balances that support, rather than erode, high levels of trust.

Many organizations overreact to cases of deception or incompetence; they design systems that place excessive controls on the 99 percent of the people who can actually be trusted. These controls institutionalize distrust, and the organization, its members, and ultimately its customers suffer as a result. This is not the answer.

The types of control used in the past—a formal hierarchy, rigid policies and procedures, restricted information flow, and narrow functional specialization—are also not well suited to today's competitive demands. Instead, we are starting to see new forms of control that are self-designed and collectively owned.

These checks and balances, including forms of monitoring, auditing, and managing performance, need to be consistent with the culture that an organization is striving to develop. For example, traditional approaches to control in a highly empowered organization will ultimately fail, either by being ignored or by eroding the culture that the firm is trying to create.

❧

A Framework for Building Trust

It is nearly impossible to find complete trust or distrust. Complete distrust would be too great a burden, and complete trust would be too great a risk. The kind of distrust that is manifested as a general unwillingness to expect competence or concern on the part of those on whom one depends is undoubtedly destructive. Yet we must recognize the important functions of safeguards and strive to provide "supportive" control mechanisms that allow trust to grow.

The stories of Barings and General Motors are headline grabbers because they suggest the vulnerability of once-great organizations. In many respects, they illustrate the difficult balance between trusting too much and trusting not at all. They help underscore the importance of developing and sustaining trust in the new competitive environment. Trust has become ever more important because it helps us manage complexity, fosters a capacity for action, enhances collaboration, and increases organizational learning.

As we examine ways to encourage and manage trust, we must recognize that no foolproof handbook is available for those seeking to develop this elusive and increasingly important factor in organizational performance. Trust is not something one changes with pronouncements or good intentions. Seeking to improve trust directly, in fact, can result in higher levels of suspicion if the process is not managed effectively.

The key imperatives in building high-trust organizations and teams are achieving results, acting with integrity, and demonstrating concern, as shown in Figure 1.2. Sustaining an appropriate level of trust requires balancing these imperatives—even when they come into conflict with each other. This balancing act requires superb leadership as well as an organization designed to sustain trust (including both the formal organizational architecture and the informal culture).

Figure 1.2. Building Trust.

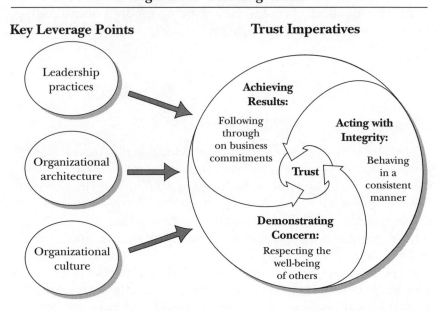

In the following chapter, we introduce the three trust impera-tives and demonstrate more clearly the importance of trust to the success of an organization.

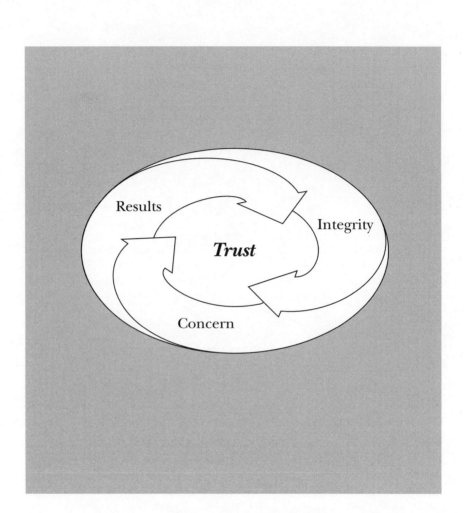

Chapter Two

Defining Trust: The Basics

The word *trust* is derived from the German word *trost,* which suggests comfort. It begins with an assessment of another's capabilities or character. In most cases, we trust those who demonstrate they are worthy of it. Yet trust is not always rooted in past experience with others. This is how trust is distinguished from confidence. Confidence arises as a result of specific knowledge; it is built on reason and fact. In contrast, trust is based, in part, on faith. We sometimes give our trust in spite of evidence that might suggest we should feel some caution, if not outright suspicion, about relying on another.

Trust, however, is not absolute faith. In its most extreme forms, faith can be seen as a belief that is largely immune to contradictory information or events. Pure faith is beyond reason: those with such faith can justify any event or view, even if it conflicts with their worldview; this is what we mean by "blind faith." Faith is resistant to change even when the price of having faith, of being a "believer," is detrimental to the faithful. But trust is commonly understood as being more fragile than faith. Trust can be broken more readily—and by events of considerably less significance—than faith. The possibility of withdrawing the trust we place in others—and of others withdrawing their trust in us—is very real.

Trust, then, is more than simple confidence and less than blind faith. As a working definition of trust, I use the following:

> *Trust:* Belief that those on whom we depend will meet our expectations of them

We trust those who meet our expectations. It is more accurate, however, to say we trust those who meet our positive expectations. Someone who is intent on harming us may fulfill our expectations (we expect the worst from him or her and we get it), yet we cannot say we *trust* this person. Instead, when we trust others, we assume that they will behave in a manner consistent with our interests (as far as is possible). In short, we come to believe that those we trust are both willing and able to meet our needs.

Trust thus hinges on our assessment of another's capacity to meet our needs. We evaluate people's trustworthiness in relation to what we expect from them. These expectations, both explicit and implicit, influence the specific point at which we extend our trust, temper it, withhold it, or withdraw it.

Understanding another's expectations is therefore essential in determining how best to build a trusting relationship. Expectations that have been made explicit are the simple part of the equation. We expect, for example, someone to deliver on a project commitment that is clearly stated and understood. Trust builds when people follow through on these specified commitments, and it erodes when they do not.

But the implicit or "background" expectations are the ones that create the unseen land mines in the process of establishing and maintaining trust. For instance, in some firms people expect lifetime employment, even though no one has actually provided such a guarantee. In fact, employees may hold this expectation even when leadership has told them that success in the marketplace is the only way to ensure job security. Background expectations such as these are taken for granted until an event (such as a reduction in the workforce) makes them explicit.

This is not to suggest that simply knowing and fulfilling expectations sustains trust. Malevolence and incompetence, even when they are expected or anticipated, will thoroughly undermine trust. More often, though, it is inconsistency between what one expects and what one observes that raises doubts about the motives or ability of those in whom we place our trust.

The Need for Vulnerability

Trust becomes an issue when others have significant influence over something that is important to us. Whether deciding whom we will marry, forming a business partnership, or selecting a physician to cure our child's disease, each of us wonders if the risk associated with our trust is worth the potential benefit we will derive from it. Our cautious assessment of another's intentions and capabilities always falls short of complete certainty: we cannot be guaranteed that our trust is warranted any more than we can predict the future.

Consider, for example, the plight of CEO Hugh McColl. After building NationsBank into one of the country's financial power-houses, he now faces a new set of challenges that are remaking the banking industry. The driving force behind these changes is tech-nology, and McColl is aware that he lacks the mastery needed to play the kind of hands-on leadership role that he has in the past with his firm's many acquisitions and deals. As a result, McColl is increasingly forced to rely on others, particularly those with tech-nology backgrounds. Rather than make decisions with a small cir-cle of advisers and then quickly move forward, he must now rely on others to drive the bank's new technology strategy. McColl notes, "I'm more dependent on others than I have ever been in my life. It doesn't feel good."[1]

Trust is central in situations that have the potential for signifi-cant negative outcomes; its importance increases in proportion to the degree of our dependence on others. For example, those who must depend on the work of others to meet their business objec-tives require significant trust. The potential harm of depending on an untrustworthy colleague can quickly outweigh the benefits of collaboration. Risk of this sort and the associated trust are unnec-essary for those who can control all aspects of their work. But those who work on complicated projects, which may involve people from different parts of the world, have no option but to rely on others. So how do we both offer our trust and limit our risks?

As we give trust and thus become vulnerable, we are partic-ularly attuned to acts that reflect on the trustworthiness of another. It bears repeating: trust grows when we rely on others who, over time, fulfill our expectations. It fades and turns into distrust when those on whom we rely fail to meet our expecta-tions. Each person determines how much he or she is willing to risk at various points in an evolving relationship. Most of us man-age the vulnerability associated with trust by taking only small risks in our initial relationship with others; this provides an opportunity to test to see if our trust is warranted. For example, partners in new alliances often commit to each other by degrees. Only after they have observed their new partners in action do they make a long-term commitment to joint efforts. Although this trial period does not offer complete assurance that everyone in the alliance is trustworthy, it does provide an opportunity to gain more information about each other and about the wisdom of working together.

Risking Trust

One of the paradoxes of trust is that trust cannot grow unless we take risks that may result in distrust. In other words, we must risk being wrong if we are ever to determine whether we are right in giving our trust. In a world of identical interests and capabilities, the risks associated with trust would be minimal and the process would be as natural as breathing. But since the interests of people often differ, as do their abilities to meet our needs, trust becomes more problematic. Without risks, there is no need for trust. Trust and risk give rise to each other; it is rare to find one without the other.

Consider, for example, the individual who has just learned that she has leukemia. On the advice of her family doctor, she goes to a university hospital for treatment. The life-threatening nature of the illness means that her choice of therapy is critical. She can choose a traditional therapeutic approach with a proven survival rate of 50 percent. Or she can become part of a research trial for a new medication that has yet to be proven effective. She is told that the hospital would like her to try the new treatment because of the potential for a better outcome. This situation requires trust because the sick individual must confront the risk of losing her life. She is forced to trust others in areas where she has limited knowledge and experience. What are her chances of survival if she foregoes all treatment out of distrust of the medical establishment? Should she get a second opinion? A third? Does the hospital, which has a reputation for being on the leading edge of leukemia research, care more about the clinical trial than about her well-being? Should she trust a cadre of doctors, many of them young and none of whom she has ever met? Are they the best available for her particular disease? As the months pass, how will she know if the trust she has placed in them has been warranted? If she is wrong in following their advice, will it be too late to try another treatment? How will she come to a decision?

To Trust or Not?

Most of us enter into situations of trust with trepidation; the degree of fear varies with each individual and circumstance. Many people tend to view others as either trustworthy or untrustworthy, with no middle ground; they treat the choice between trust and distrust as an either-or decision in order to reduce life's complexity. Each of us has our own limits of trust, and once these are violated, we become distrustful. But the point at which trust becomes distrust also depends on each situation. Trusting one's friend is somewhat different from trusting one's business partner (since we depend on these people in different ways). The same acts that may result in distrusting one's business partner, for example, would have little or no bearing on distrusting our friend. A friend's lack of knowledge of the complexities of our work would have no bearing on our trust, but if our business colleague didn't have this knowledge, we would not rely on her to perform work-related tasks. By the same token, if a friend consistently ignores the problems we are having in our personal life, our trust will begin to erode; whether a business colleague understands these issues will most likely not influence our trust in her or his ability to perform a task that is important to the business. Our dependencies on others vary, and, therefore, the reasons for which our trust will be broken do as well.

Thresholds of Trust

People have different trust thresholds based on their experiences; the point at which trust becomes distrust depends on the individuals involved. For example, some patients will never return to a physician who misdiagnoses a potentially life-threatening disease. This one mistake—with the potential for enormous consequences—makes it impossible for the patient to rely on the doctor's advice, even if this was one mistake out of a thousand decisions.

Similarly, some people bring an immediate end to a business partnership if a partner breaches on an agreement. For them, a

single dramatic act, particularly early in the relationship, irrevoca-
bly undermines any trust that may have developed. Others look for
ways to repair the breach of trust and salvage the partnership. This
is not to say that their trust hasn't been undermined. It may be that
their commitment to the partnership itself or the success of the
business demands an attempt to reestablish trust. Or it may be that
their threshold of trust (or their expectations of a partner's behavior) differ from those who would end the partnership.

This is how one individual interviewed for this book commented
on trust:

> My daddy used to say that you trust them or you don't. I was in
> the navy during World War II and had a man reporting to me who
> was responsible for maintaining a gun mount. One day, I saw him
> throw some parts over the side of the ship. He was looking to see
> if anyone was watching before he did it. I took his gun apart and
> found that he had left some parts out after he cleaned it. Not
> knowing what to do with them and unwilling to admit he didn't
> know what he was doing, he tossed them overboard. I could not
> trust him anymore after that. Guns are very important and it was
> impossible for me to keep an eye on him all day. I transferred
> him out of my unit.

In this context—a potentially life-or-death situation involving many
people—the absolute distrust seems warranted. Yet distrust and trust
must be tempered to fit the people and circumstances involved.

A "trust threshold" (as shown in Figure 2.1) helps protect us
from the untrustworthy. Without some point at which we withdraw
our trust, we would expose ourselves to risks that could harm us as
individuals or harm the groups to which we belong. Each individual, team, and organization has a point at which it will withdraw its
trust of others.

Once broached, a threshold blocks the rebuilding of trust. This
is one way of understanding how distrust often appears to be self-
perpetuating: the suspicious find reasons to reinforce their lack of
confidence in others. Even if the individual or group who violated
our trust changes, it is all too easy to discount or explain away these
positive actions. To be fooled again would hurt too much or entail
too much risk. Every new error, however unintentional, becomes
one more piece of evidence that the conciliatory effort is merely a

Figure 2.1. Trust Threshold.

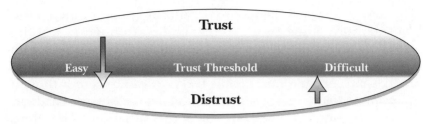

"Trust—Difficult to regain once lost"

sham and that nothing has really changed. It is possible to get out of such a cycle, but the potential for rebuilding a trusting relationship can quickly slip away.

Three factors are important in the establishment of a threshold: the situation, those giving their trust, and those asking to be trusted.

- *The Situation.* Depending on the risk involved, some situations require a higher or lower threshold of trust. The fundamental question, "Do you trust them?" always exists in relation to a more specific question: "Trust them to do what?"[2] A key strategic partnership, for example, requires more trust than a meeting between two companies to share their best practices. Those involved in setting up a partnership may establish a higher threshold of trust because of the risks involved should the partner prove untrustworthy.

- *Those Giving Their Trust.* Based on their own history and temperament, individuals, teams, and organizations are inclined to establish higher or lower trust thresholds. If, for example, one of the firms in a strategic partnership has had a bad partnership experience in the past, people in that firm will be more likely to set high thresholds to try to avoid repeating the earlier mistake.

- *Those Asking to Be Trusted.* Depending on the perceived credibility of those we are considering trusting, we may raise or lower the trust threshold we use. Those with a highly credible reputation may be given more leeway than those with a negative reputation or those whom we do not know. A strategic partner, for example, who has built a number of long-term and mutually beneficial relationships with other firms is more likely to be given the benefit of any doubts as a new partnership forms.

Radius of Trust

The degree to which people in organizations trust others varies considerably. Some firms, for example, are open to working closely with outside organizations in collaborative ventures. Others are highly suspicious of anyone from another organization, or, in some corporations, people feel they can trust only those in their immediate work group. Thus the degree of trust varies not only across organizations but also across situations. The things we need to trust range from those closest to us (I can trust that my fellow team members will not sabotage my efforts when I am out of the office) to the everyday interactions that make up our business lives (I can trust that the memo I just received is factual and complete).

When we trust others, we don't need to monitor their actions or question every variation from what we expect. If I trust my partner, then I can go on a business trip and think about my presentations and meetings rather than worry about my partner's actions. I can act on the information contained in the memo and not worry about whether it contains some hidden agenda or distortion. With trust, life becomes much simpler. With trust, we can devote our attention to a much broader range of activities than would be possible in an environment of suspicion.

Trust, however, comes with a price. The more we trust, the more we risk disappointment, if not harm. Trust increases our vulnerability to others; distrust decreases that vulnerability. We thus face competing needs. We want to simplify a complex world, build supportive relationships, and take on additional risks through trust. We want to trust because it is far easier, less demanding, and offers more possibilities than chronic suspicion. Without trust, we would be "prey to a vague sense of dread, to paralyzing fears. . . . Such abrupt confrontation with the complexity of the world is beyond human endurance."[3] We seek to reduce our vulnerability to others through distrust. We need to protect ourselves from those who have the potential to harm us. We thus struggle to balance a healthy level of trust with a necessary level of distrust.

Since in order to function in the world, we each must trust others to some degree, the questions facing all of us as individuals—and as members of teams, organizations, and society—are

- How much do we trust others in general?
- Whom do we trust in specific situations?

Our answers to these questions can help us assess the degree to which we trust others. They can also help us determine the degree to which our team or organization is willing to trust others in the pursuit of business objectives. In both cases, we can envision a set of overlapping circles that encompasses the people we are willing to trust. The radius of these circles extends outward from individuals to team members, other organizational members, and those who are not part of the organization but who come into contact with its members (this may include suppliers and partners in alliances). Those with a restricted radius of trust are unwilling or unable to trust many others. The most extreme case of this is the paranoid who trusts no one; indeed, some paranoids do not even trust themselves. In a business setting, a restricted radius of trust might include only oneself and one's fellow team members (see Figure 2.2).

In contrast, an expansive radius of trust suggests a willingness to trust people outside of one's immediate work group or organization. This means that trust would extend outward from self to team members, to other organizational members, to those outside of the organization (see Figure 2.3). A radius of trust can also vary so that some groups are more trusted than others. For example, members of a manufacturing group may trust those in a quality assurance group more than they trust those in sales and marketing.

Results, Integrity, and Concern

What can be done to expand the radius of trust in organizations? In other words, what actions can leaders take to create the trust needed in today's rapidly changing marketplace? To build high-performance corporations, we need to understand the key leverage points that give rise to trust. Research, as well as my experience as a management consultant, indicates that trust is founded on a few basic imperatives: achieving results, acting with integrity, and demonstrating concern.[4] For high levels of trust to exist, these factors must be exhibited and practiced consistently.

Figure 2.2. Restricted Trust Radius.

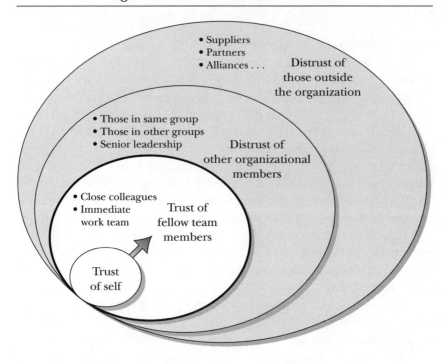

Achieving Results

The first and perhaps most important imperative in earning trust in a business setting—or indeed, in any setting that demands action and results—involves people's performance in fulfilling their obligations and commitments. The results are key: even if people's motives are characterized by goodwill, they will not retain our trust if they are incompetent or powerless to fulfill the expectations we have of them. In such cases, we deem them unworthy of trust not because they are malicious but because they can't deliver. For example, when we rely on a surgeon in the operating room, we are more interested in her skill and competence as a professional than in her level of personal concern; when an employee says, "I have total trust in our senior leadership team to prepare our organization for the future; they are the best," he is basing his trust on the issue of competence and the ability to produce results.

Figure 2.3. Expansive Trust Radius.

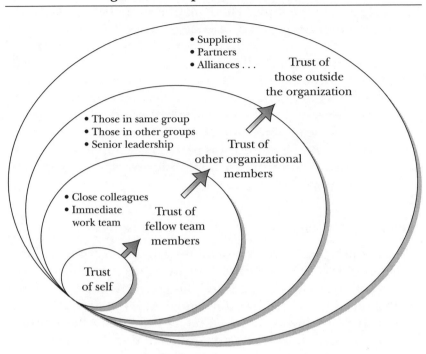

Acting with Integrity

A second imperative for trust is acting with integrity. By integrity, we mean honesty in one's words and consistency in one's actions. In most cases, we trust those who behave consistently in their words and actions, who truly live by the motto of "do what you say you will do."[5] If, for example, we see inconsistency in another's words or deeds, we may conclude that he is at odds with our interests or unable to fulfill his professional responsibilities. Even the perception of inconsistency (which may not have a factual basis) can result in increasing our distrust.

Trust requires that our most important expectations in a given situation be fulfilled. Gaps between what we anticipate and what actually occurs give rise to distrust. Imagine that you have loaned a large sum of money to a friend who promises to repay the amount in two months. Time passes and the loan is not repaid. As more time passes, you are likely to begin to distrust, questioning why the loan is outstanding. There may be a number of sound reasons for the delay, but in the absence of an explanation, you will begin to question your friend's motives and become suspicious.

Inconsistency suggests that others may be dishonest and self-serving and thus unworthy of trust. Inconsistency in words and actions is one of the most important indicators we have that others are incompetent or perhaps malevolent—and it is these attributes that often mean others will not fulfill their obligations to us. The impact of integrity on trust is particularly important early in the history of a relationship, as each side assesses the degree to which it is willing to risk vulnerability.

Demonstrating Concern

A third imperative for trust is demonstrating concern for others. At the most basic level, we trust those who care about us. We trust those whom we believe understand our concerns and will act in a way that meets or at least does not conflict with our needs. This element of concern involves the degree to which we believe others are supporting our own well-being or that of the whole. For example, trust is evident in this statement: "He is not working any personal agenda and wants what is best for the company."

We expect those we trust to remain loyal to our interests even if future events provide an incentive to do otherwise. In other words, the imperative of concern requires that those we trust be responsive to our needs even in the face of potentially conflicting pressures. It does not require that those we trust subjugate their own needs in all situations, but we do assume that these individuals will not deliberately hurt us or take advantage of our reliance on them. Expressions that suggest this component of trust include such statements as "I would trust her with my money," "I could tell him anything and know that he would not betray me," or "She has helped me at every stage of my career and has been a true mentor."

Concern for others as an imperative for trust goes beyond caring for us as individuals; it includes a broader concern for the groups of which we are part. We expect those we trust to extend their concern to our family, our work team, or our company. This is particularly important in relation to trusting those in positions of leadership and authority, as their concern or lack of it can have an impact not only on individuals but on larger groups as well.

The Balancing Act

To sustain trust, organizations must achieve results, act with integrity, and demonstrate concern. The dilemma is that these three imperatives can conflict with each other. Managing the ongoing tension among them is essential but difficult. Actions leaders must take in order to fulfill their responsibilities and thus act competently may violate the need to demonstrate concern. A leader, for example, may need to reengineer her firm to remain competitive, but in doing so, she may have to let thousands of people go. How well or poorly the reengineering process is managed will have an impact on employee perceptions of her concern. But no matter how well done, the act of terminating thousands of people will result in the perception that the leader does not care about the workforce (or does not care as much about the workforce as about bottom-line financial results). In this case, the need to achieve results is, at least in terms of perception, at odds with the need to demonstrate concern.

Trust is also based on perceptions of consistency in our actions and words. In most cases, trust declines when we act inconsistently and fail to follow through on our commitments. Yet the nature of today's business environment makes commitments increasingly short-lived as conditions call for rapid changes in a firm's strategy and policy. This may mean that an organization's direction will be in constant flux. As a result, employees may come to believe that the organization and its leaders are failing to follow through on their stated intentions. The need to act responsibly may well mean shifting direction, but this may damage credibility regarding consistency. Some leaders attempt to deal with this dilemma by not clearly communicating their intentions in the first place, just in case those intentions need to change as the environment changes. The result, of course, is that employees feel they are not being given the information they need about the firm's direction and strategic imperatives. All told, there is no easy answer to the trust dilemmas created by shifts in strategy and direction.

The relative importance of each trust imperative varies with the situation. Some circumstances require a greater emphasis on one element; for example, a crisis situation may require a greater focus on results and less on concern. Still, the absence of one or more of the three imperatives can result over time in low levels of overall trust, even if the other two are present. As a consequence, when we think of trust as an equation, we can see that organizations must perform sufficiently in each of the three areas in order to achieve and sustain trust (see Figure 2.4).

Thus, the trust imperatives influence each other; extremely low scores on results, integrity, or concern can overwhelm progress in the other areas and undermine trust. Leaders who achieve results but who do so in a way that lacks integrity will not be trusted—even though they have delivered the results expected of them. The formula also suggests how trust can be sustained when performance is poor (but not disastrous) in one area but high in the other two areas. For example, leaders can sometimes overcome the perception of inconsistency in their actions if they deliver results and demonstrate concern for people. In other words, people will *sometimes* overlook shortcomings in one area, within certain limits of acceptability, if performance in the other two areas is especially strong. But these cases are usually exceptions.

⋞⫘⋟

Monitoring Trust

We manage the risks that come with depending on others by assessing—and constantly reassessing—their trustworthiness. In this way, we are able to balance the need to simplify a complex world and

Figure 2.4. Achieving and Sustaining Trust.

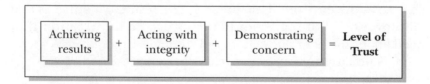

build supportive relationships through trust with the need to reduce our vulnerability through distrust and other mechanisms that help protect us from undesirable outcomes. This is particularly important for those in leadership positions who need both to trust others and to ensure that such trust is warranted.

Most of us attempt to qualify our trust based on a sound assessment of others' willingness and ability to meet the expectations we have of them. The key imperatives—achieving results, acting with integrity, and demonstrating concern for others—help explain our assessments of another's trustworthiness. In addition, these imperatives may determine why some organizations develop appropriate levels of trust while others find themselves being too restricted (from trusting too little) or too vulnerable (from trusting too much).

In this chapter, we have begun to look at the following questions:

- What enables us, in general, to trust others?
- How can we, as individuals, learn to behave in ways that increase the likelihood of others trusting us?
- How can we build organizations and teams with the trust needed to compete effectively?
- What is the limit of our trust? How do we establish necessary safeguards to ensure that our trust is not abused?

In Part Two, we delve deeper into these questions and look in turn at each of the three imperatives.

Trust Survey

Assessing Your Organization or Team

To assess the degree of trust in your organization or team, complete the following survey. The contrasting statements are designed to provoke your thinking regarding the level of trust that currently exists. For each statement, indicate which point along the continuum most accurately describes your organization or team. The total at the bottom of the page provides a general measure of trust; the ratings on individual questions provide more detailed feedback. You can use your ratings to identify areas that need improvement.

Transfer your ratings on the surveys at the end of each of the next three chapters to Resource One to develop a complete trust profile of your organization or team.

Exhibiting Trust

Assessing Your Organization or Team

In this organization (or team) . . .

Power and control are in the hands of a few individuals or groups		People at all levels feel and act like "owners" of the business
"Warfare" among the different groups is common		Different groups (HQ, functions, units) work together collaboratively
People play it safe and make sure they don't get caught failing		People are willing to take personal risks in order to help the business grow
People support the status quo and resist change		People are open to change and new ways of operating
People will not express their true thoughts or feelings		People feel free to express their views even if different from those of the majority
No one takes responsibility for mistakes and we repeat them over time		We are open about our mistakes and learn from them
There are many controls and restrictions on what people can do		People are given the freedom they need to do their jobs
Overall, there is very little trust within the organization		Overall, there is a great deal of trust within the organization

Total Score: _____

Low trust: 8–18; Moderate trust: 19–29; High trust: 30–40

The Imperatives of Trust

Results, Integrity, Concern

Part Two examines the key imperatives required to sustain trust in organizations. My intent is to provide a pragmatic model that offers leaders a way to understand and influence the level of trust within their organizations and teams.

In the three chapters of this section, I highlight several key themes:

1. Trust requires fulfillment of the results promised to others. Many make the mistake of viewing trust as a soft issue that is detached from hard business realities. Trust, however, requires that we believe that others are willing and able to meet their commitments to us.

2. Trust requires integrity in following a known set of values, beliefs, and practices. In other words, trust depends on consistency and coherence in one's statements and actions. This is sometimes called "walking the talk" or "modeling the message." Failures of integrity call into question the trustworthiness of others.

3. Trust requires concern for the well-being of others. This does not mean that the interests of others always come before our own or before those of the organization as a whole. It does, however, suggest the importance of understanding the impact of one's actions on others. Concern also reflects a sincere desire

to promote the well-being and success of people at all levels of the organization.

The ideas presented in Chapters Three, Four, and Five form the core of this book. They provide a way of understanding how trust is won or lost.

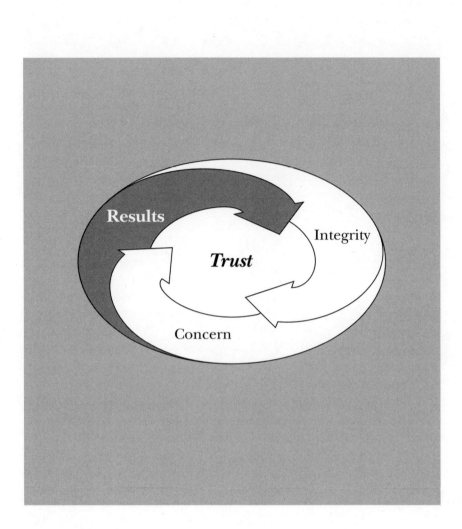

Chapter Three

| Achieving Business Results

Vincent Gargano, a resident of Chicago, was recently undergoing chemotherapy for cancer. He was told by his doctors that he was making significant progress and would shortly be able to return home. But then he was accidentally given an overdose of an anti-cancer medication—and died in the hospital. In writing out a drug prescription for Gargano, a resident doctor had reversed the amounts of two drugs. As a result, for nearly a week Gargano received a dose of one drug that was four times too high. He suffered a number of side effects from the overdose, including progressive hearing loss, kidney failure, and festering sores as his immune system weakened. A lawyer for Gargano's family said, "There are dozens of people who should have caught this mistake. The whole system just fell apart."[1]

Instances of medical malpractice surface almost weekly in our local newspapers. In such cases, those who trusted their physicians have their faith destroyed due to negligence or incompetence. Similarly, we see cases of malpractice in many businesses. These may not be life threatening, but their impact is widely felt. Mistakes, particularly those of major proportions, threaten the success of the firm and, in extreme cases, the security of its employees and the well-being of the larger community within which it operates.

Look, for example, at the problems the once powerful Digital Equipment Corporation had in the early nineties. Sales were drying up in its key minicomputer line. A two-year-old restructuring plan had failed miserably. Forecasting and production-planning systems had broken down. Cost cutting hadn't come close to restoring profitability. Top executives—including a handful of outsiders recruited for a turnaround—bolted. A long-term strategy to rebuild around a hot new chip wasn't paying off. Instead, the firm went through several rounds of significant layoffs, and more are likely for the near future. Shareholders suffered as the firm failed to meet financial expectations.[2] Due to the mistakes of Ken Olson and his leadership team during the 1980s, DEC has been in crisis through most of this decade. While some progress has been made over the past few years, DEC recently announced another financial shortfall in its PC business. Seven thousand people will lose their jobs as the firm undergoes a $500 million restructuring. A number of senior-level executives have departed this year, and the stock has declined more than 10 percent. Some believe that DEC will never recover its status as one of our premier computer companies and that at best it will become a second-tier company.[3]

DEC, of course, is not alone. The turmoil at Apple under the leadership of recently departed CEO Michael Spindler makes DEC's look like a relatively mild case of leadership malpractice. Apple missed many strategic opportunities. The firm failed, for example, to license its superior operating system in the late 1980s and early 1990s and allowed Micosoft to close the performance gap with its newly released Windows 95. Had Apple licensed its operating system, it would probably have taken a dominant position in the global computer market—instead of reporting stunning quarterly losses. Apple also misfired in its operational decisions, as evidenced by a backlog inventory amounting to over $1 billion—a mistake that resulted from overforecasting demand.

Similarly, the lack of trust in Frank Borman at Eastern and in Roger Smith at General Motors arose, at least in part, because both men made strategic mistakes that forced employees to question their leaders' ability. The result was an erosion of the trust needed to get a firm through difficult times.

When asked about trust in leadership in his organization, one employee of a Fortune 500 firm told me:

> In the past few years, I've developed an almost total lack of faith and trust in the management of this company. At times it's like being on a ship without a helmsman, being driven about by every whim of the wind and the waves. Decisions are made without factual input, or more often decisions or direction is delayed until the time for action is long past.

The distrust that is created when organizational members, and leaders in particular, fail to deliver results is pervasive. Employees begin to question their commitment to a company that is failing in the marketplace. They also begin to question whether they should follow the strategic direction of leaders who have made a series of damaging blunders. Consider the following comments I heard from employees in firms suffering from bad decisions and flawed implementation efforts:

> I'm not sure this company knows what it is or what it wants to be, and it's just made too many wrong decisions in the past few months.

> Our management is too reactionary, and they don't anticipate. We just do things by trial and error: no thought, no planning, even when you could see things coming for a long time. It doesn't breed trust because it doesn't seem that the top management knows what it is doing.

> When people begin to sense that management is not making wise or even prudent decisions, they start to have a lack of faith and trust in top management. This reorganization dragged on and on, and you couldn't pinpoint who was captain of the boat. Nobody would admit responsibility for decisions or answer any questions.

As these quotes suggest, achieving results is particularly important for leadership's credibility. Indeed, the first component of trust is to deliver the results needed for one's firm to grow and prosper.

In today's high-performance organization, however, these demands fall not just on leaders. Every person must deliver the expected results or the organization will fail to keep pace with its competition. It is no longer sufficient for a few key people to perform in order for the enterprise to grow and prosper. Indeed, as Wayne Calloway, former CEO of Pepsi has said, "we look at the results people achieve. Did they make the business grow? Did they develop the people they supervise? Did they find a new, better way to accomplish an old, familiar task? Did they raise the level of quality? Improve the level of efficiency? Did they get the job done on time, on budget?"[4]

Achieving results applies to individuals, teams, and organizations. Follow-through at each level is the core of running a corporation. Trust cannot develop fully unless the business is run in a manner that produces consistently positive results. While this seems obvious, most people, when asked about the factors that build trust, mention the interpersonal aspects. In a recent talk, I asked eighty people to describe the factors that undermine trust in their organizations. Their feedback described, in large part, the psychological impact of downsizing and various forms of inconsistency on the part of leadership in failing to "walk the talk." None of the session participants mentioned the importance of people at all levels meeting their business obligations to each other, to customers, and to shareholders. This "hard" side of trust is as important as—and in some cases, more important than—the "softer" elements (such as caring about and understanding others) that typically come to mind.

Consider the recent events at IBM. The firm that once dominated its industry and was seen as a model of modern management practices became plagued in the late eighties and early nineties by eroding market share and declining margins. By the time Lou Gerstner was brought in to revitalize the organization, the confidence of the once proud firm had already been shaken. Gerstner was an outsider with no industry experience; no doubt many within the organization questioned his ability to lead the firm. Yet over a several-year period, he has led a turnaround that is reflected in almost every performance statistic. Gerstner's credibility required that he achieve concrete results. Otherwise, any talk on his part about integrity or concern would have been largely superficial, and he would not have gained the trust of his employees.

Leaders in similar situations must be aware that whether or not they deliver results has an impact on trust. In a business context, trust is always tied to the need to deliver on commitments—beginning with the commitment to create sufficient profits and shareholder return.

Achieving Predictable Outcomes

Thus, trust requires that those on whom we depend deliver the results we expect from them. The nature of these results varies depending on the organization and the specific challenges it faces. In the most general sense, delivering results is simply delivering what others expect of us. These people include customers, those we report to, fellow employees, associates, and shareholders. Customers look for results that reflect product quality, service quality, and the perceived value of products and services. They also look for new products and services. Results in these areas tend to increase customer loyalty and customer satisfaction. Supervisors as well as fellow employees and associates are often concerned with improvements in core business processes and mechanisms to enhance learning and increase employee skill and knowledge. Shareholders expect results with respect to revenue and profit targets, growth within new markets or product lines, and efficiency and productivity goals.

To the extent that organizations empower business units, teams, and individuals, leaders are increasingly forced to trust that others will deliver on their commitments. This makes senior leaders more vulnerable than ever: they are more dependent on others and have far less control than in the past around the delivery of results. Those who are unable to deliver the results expected of them will be deemed unworthy of trust not because they are malicious but because they don't have the ability to deliver what is needed.

The Goal: Winning in the Marketplace

Hewlett-Packard today employs almost thirty thousand more people than it did a decade ago. In contrast, over that same period, IBM has shed half of its workforce. Hewlett-Packard has achieved superb short-term financial results even as it positions itself to take advantage of new growth markets. In declaring Hewlett-Packard the performer of the year for 1995, *Forbes* magazine noted that "for those who entrusted their careers to it as well as to those who entrusted their investment, HP has delivered."[5]

HP's business success is partially attributed to its innovative human resource practices—that is, its willingness to experiment with new ways of organizing and managing people. Yet those who are familiar with the firm understand that its success is due, in large part, to a desire to make a contribution through the development of innovative products. There is also a passion for winning in the marketplace and earning a profit. David Packard, in reflecting on the evolution of the firm that he created with Bill Hewlett, observed that some analysts have neglected the importance of winning in HP's culture. In fact, as he said, their "strong desire to win . . . was probably more important than all the other things. We were determined to do what we had to do to be the best; that was our underlying program."[6]

As the firm's corporate objectives says:

> In our economic system, the profit we generate from our operations is the ultimate source of the funds we need to prosper and grow. It is the one absolutely essential measure of our corporate performance over the long-term. Only if we continue to meet our profit objectives can we achieve our other corporate objectives. . . . Profit is not something that can be put off until tomorrow; it must be achieved today. It means that myriad jobs be done correctly and efficiently. The day-to-day performance of each individual adds to—or subtracts from—our profit. Profit is the responsibility of all.[7]

The need for results is even more pronounced in situations of turmoil. Ironically, redirecting a firm that is in trouble may require actions that don't build trust in the short run. The senior leader may well need to take control and demonstrate progress in getting the business fundamentals right before empowering others to act. In other cases, a participative approach will be more constructive. But either way, there must be an emphasis on business performance. Talking about trust when the company is failing is contradictory.

Lou Gerstner underscores this point with his belief that other positive organizational factors all depend on IBM's short-term and long-term success in the marketplace. In other words, you can't rebuild trust in a place like IBM unless people have confidence in your ability to win in the marketplace. As results improve, employees become more confident that leadership's competitive vision of IBM's role will work and enable the firm to grow. Strong business fundamentals are the foundation of trust. High levels of trust are rarely found in situations of rapidly declining market share. While this sounds self-evident, many leaders talk about the soft side of organizational life before they deal with the hard realities of the marketplace.

Trust begins with the development of a viable business model and a demonstration of success through the use of that model. Working directly on the soft side of organizational performance is futile if the business model is fundamentally flawed. As Jack Welch of GE has noted, "in the end, you and your associates . . . have to create an atmosphere where customers want what you're delivering or all the speeches about loyalty and trust won't mean a thing."[8]

A results-driven company has a number of attributes that distinguish it from other firms. The list includes the following:

- *Establish clear, ambitious performance targets.* Precise targets help make it clear how each individual and team within the organization can contribute directly to the firm's success. Targets also clarify the larger competitive context in which people are working and the results expected from each area of the organization.

- *Expect superb execution of initiatives.* Provide the support (information, training, and resources) to help ensure superior execution of the tasks expected by customers, employees, and shareholders.

- *Provide consequences for success and failure.* Evenhandedly and consistently enforce performance consequences at the individual, team, and organizational levels.

Establishing Clear, Ambitious Performance Targets

Most people familiar with General Electric would agree that the firm is obsessed with performance. Since Welch became CEO in the early 1980s, there has been a pervasive emphasis on maximizing shareholder value. Over the past decade, GE's performance has been second only to Coca-Cola in increasing shareholder value. At GE, most believe that employees are evaluated based on performance as measured against a clear set of objectives and not (as in some other firms) on political factors or personal loyalties. As Steve Kerr, vice president of corporate management development at GE, told me:

> At GE, we spend a great deal of time articulating the outputs we expect from our businesses and people. Most of our time is spent agreeing on the improvement we expect in each critical area. Once that is done, we trust our people to find a way to make those targets. In other words, our efforts go into gaining clear agreement on the outputs rather than the means of achieving the outputs.

Welch, for example, doesn't get involved in operational issues. Instead, he pays attention to the overall goals and the strategic issues we need to face as a corporation.

> Goal congruence is critical in establishing a culture of trust. . . . Our performance-driven culture requires a certain degree of sophistication about targets and the myriad of factors that can influence outcomes. For example, we pay a great deal of attention to inventory turns, but in some of our businesses (such as aviation) the turns are low because of the nature of the business. Therefore, we are careful to understand the limits of our own obsessiveness around performance and hard measures.

In an era of downsizing, the performance focus at GE has been particularly important. It gives employees confidence that their performance is evaluated against a set of known standards. Because they understand how they will be evaluated and rewarded, employees feel they have a measure of control in today's uncertain business world.

Expecting Superb Execution of Initiatives

A second trait found in results-driven firms is attention to the details of executing new strategies. Ongoing attention to a "vital few" priorities is essential. These critical initiatives become the mantras of senior leaders; they express the priorities that help create a culture in which everyone assumes responsibility for the firm's winning in the marketplace and delivering the results expected by customers, shareholders, and employees.

For example, the pharmaceutical firm Pfizer is recognized as one of the best in its industry. It has one of the strongest research and development groups in the world and has demonstrated an ability to capture market share in new drug categories. In talking about the role of leadership, William Steer, Pfizer's CEO, notes:

> A key part of the leader's role is to ensure that appropriate monitoring and follow-up systems are in place to remind the organization of its key priorities. When employees can see and feel that management is focused, attentive and caring, as demonstrated by persistence and follow-up, the sort of constructive tension is provided that results in long-term change and continuous improvement.[9]

While the overall responsibility for the quality of implementation and for the strategic focus on execution ultimately rests with the CEO or senior team, day-to-day accountability must rest with those closest to customers and markets. Ideally, teams focused on specific customers or products assume complete responsibility for the execution of a well-delineated strategy.

Providing Consequences for Success and Failure

For the organization to prosper, much less survive, in today's marketplace, *everyone* must deliver the expected results. Trust must extend throughout the organization. The goal is thus to design our organizations systematically to sustain appropriate levels of trust relative to the risks we take in each business setting. This "new trust" has nothing to do with a soft-hearted revitalization of paternalistic practices. Nor does it mean that organizations need to be ruthless or unfair in their evaluation of performance. While such an approach may work for the short term, it cannot be sustained over a long period of time in part because of the damage it does to a firm's culture. Instead, performance consequences, both positive and negative, must be built in for individuals and for the organization at large.

Firms like Pepsi, General Electric, and Hewlett-Packard provide significant rewards and recognition for those who deliver on and then exceed their commitments. At Pepsi, for example, everyone in the firm has the opportunity to take part in stock purchases. The potential gain is significant if Pepsi's stock does well. Moreover, bonus plans reward those whose teams and business units perform well. All corporations need to be relentless in demanding superior performance of individuals, teams, and business units. And the harsh consequences that ensue when people consistently fail must be balanced—as they are at Pepsi—by significant rewards and recognition when they succeed.

Individual Performance

The larger organizations become, the greater is the opportunity for individual members to become free riders, people who benefit from being members of the organization but fail to contribute appropriately to the common effort.[10] Organizations must be tough, even ruthless, in making sure that people at all levels can be relied on to do what is required for a firm to be competitive.

Starting in the 1960s, Pepsi developed a process to "raise the bar" continually for performance standards. As David Hatch, who worked with CEO Wayne Calloway in a senior human resources function at Pepsi, told me, Calloway "was relentless on raising the bar on performance standards." Hatch saw "savvy managers come in with 10 to 12 percent revenue targets based on in-depth analysis and sound judgment about what was possible in a particular market. They would leave a meeting with Calloway agreeing to a 15 percent increase—and believing in their heart that was the right thing to do."

At Pepsi, those who fail to meet expectations are provided with feedback and an opportunity to improve. In the absence of results, they are asked to leave the company. Pepsi has demonstrated as much discipline around this process as most organizations exhibit in the realm of financial controls. For example, Calloway removed several division presidents who did not deliver results despite ample opportunity. Calloway didn't arbitrarily raise the bar. Instead, as Hatch told me, he brought people "around to a more aggressive set of goals by asking leaders about their assumptions and encouraging them to consider innovative ways to improve performance. You walked out of those meetings realizing that you did it to yourself."

Calloway knew when to be tough and when to be loose. He was tenacious on a few key issues, such as meeting targets and doing so with integrity. Otherwise, he gave his leaders tremendous autonomy and avoided the bureaucratic controls that stifle most large organizations. And the firm has balanced this tough-minded approach with a culture that places a premium on integrity and collegial support. The result of all these efforts is an exceptional firm with true competitive advantage.[11]

Similarly, despite a reputation for being an extremely supportive culture, Hewlett-Packard takes personal accountability and consequences for performance very seriously. As Bill Hewlett recalls:

> Obviously, we were very close to our employees. We understood their jobs and shared much of their lives with them. One of the most difficult steps I can remember occurred a few years after we had started the company. This was when we had to release our production manager. We finally had to face the fact that, despite everything we had done to improve his management skills, he was not

doing the job that needed to be done. Although he was a good friend, it simply came down to a question of his job or the jobs of all other employees. The impact of that decision is still with us, and in subsequent years has led us to make every effort to find an appropriate niche for a loyal employee. Interestingly enough, we have had good success through the years in relocating such employees within the company.[12]

Organizational Performance

General Electric has taken a highly visible and disciplined approach to organizational performance. In the early 1980s, Jack Welch decided to fix, close, or sell every GE business that was not first or second in worldwide market share. Under his leadership, GE sold over four hundred businesses and product lines worth $15 billion. Four layers of middle management were squeezed out. All told, Welch pushed through a massive restructuring resulting in the elimination of 170,000 jobs in ten years.

According to Welch, there was no other choice: without the cuts, GE could not have remained competitive. Welch believes that he made cuts in the 1980s to avoid cuts in the 1990s. He argues that no one person or organization can provide job security; only markets can provide security. Thus, from Welch's viewpoint, everyone must recognize that security comes only if GE is successful in the competitive marketplace.

And that marketplace was suddenly full of hungry foreign companies seeking to grab shares. This was a dramatic switch for GE, and one that demanded a change to its entire culture. As Dennis Dammerman, the senior vice president of finance at GE, reflected, no longer could the company's view toward employees be paternalistic, or even patronizing; nor could the employees anticipate "a pretty good shot at a good job for thirty or forty years and a nice retirement" by simply keeping their mouths shut and working hard.[13] The company had to focus on higher-level results—as did the employees.

Achieving Results at AlliedSignal

AlliedSignal is one of the most successful turnaround stories of this decade. Since Lawrence Bossidy became chair and CEO in 1991, net income has risen from $359 million to $875 million. Earnings per share have grown at a compound average annual rate of 25 percent. Operating margin has grown from 4.4 percent to 9.1 percent. Market value has more than doubled over the same time period. Bossidy is now attacking the one area where progress has been slower—revenue growth—and is beginning to show significant results. In its tough markets, which have mostly declined, AlliedSignal has repositioned itself to ensure growth in both profitability and revenue.[14] How have Bossidy and his team accomplished so much?

Aiming for Clear Targets

On assuming his position, Bossidy focused on a few key goals. He wanted everyone in the organization to align around these vital challenges. The organization, from his perspective, was adrift because people had no clear idea of where they were going and no feeling of progress.[15] In place of uncertainty, Bossidy created a simple change agenda. One recent year, for example, the firm's goals were to achieve its financial targets, reduce cycle times, and make growth happen. Each time Bossidy or his team visits a plant or division, they keep these goals in mind and ask if results are evident in each area.

The organization also has a few basic operating measures (productivity improvement, working capital turnover, and margins) that are closely monitored. Everyone understands that these basic measures will be used to evaluate business performance. Each measure has a specific target. For example, Bossidy pushes 6 percent productivity growth each year (with the intent of pushing costs low enough to beat any competitive bids). The consequence, over his tenure, has been some painful decisions. Twenty thousand people have lost jobs. Over $1 billion in restructuring charges were accumulated as Allied closed factories and sold off underperforming businesses. Bossidy also is pushing for 8 percent or more in annual growth in sales—and has realized this target since 1994. The challenge for Allied today is to match its productivity improvements with revenue growth.

Supporting Initiatives Through Management Processes

Four key management processes are used to run AlliedSignal:

- A strategic plan
- An operating plan
- A human resource plan
- A customer satisfaction plan[16]

The assumption is that these four key processes must be managed effectively if the company is to deliver on its growth and revenue targets.

The first review meeting is designed to develop a strategic plan for each business (within the firm's aerospace, automotive, and engineered materials groups). Allied's head of strategic planning takes charge of structuring the strategy meeting and providing necessary support to the business leaders who are making presentations. The heads of each business present key competitive issues and market share trends. Then the groups review the past year's performance as well as projections for the upcoming year. The emphasis is on what is required to meet the firm's aggressive growth targets. At the center of the discussion is a detailed analysis of competitive issues within each market segment. The group debates what can be done to move the business forward in an aggressive way and determines the best strategies for meeting their targets. Bossidy follows up each session with a short letter to the business leader that summarizes the commitments made in the meeting and the overall approach to dealing with problems.

This second management process results in detailed operational plans for each business. Allied's chief financial officer assumes overall responsibility for working with the business leaders in the development of appropriate operating plans. These, in essence, are budgets with some contingency options. The business leaders and CFO consider different future scenarios and factors that would undermine their basic assumptions about the business. Plans are then formulated to deal with any adversity that might arise, such as changes in market conditions (shifts in currency rates, for example) or problems with new product introductions. The group discusses potential actions in each case and identifies preventive measures. From his first day, Bossidy has emphasized the importance of meeting commitments. He also emphasizes the importance of treating the operational plan with the seriousness it deserves, thus ending the practice of putting together meaningless budgets.

The human resource review, the third step in the overall performance process, focuses on the organization and its people. The organizational component examines the degree to which the divisions within Allied are appropriately structured to meet customer needs and market demands. Each business is expected to develop an organizational structure that best meets the specific needs of its different customers. The second part of the review examines the status of people in the organization. The key people in each division are candidly reviewed, and their main development needs are identified. The goal is to talk directly about the people in the organization, to assess the degree to which they are meeting their goals, and to establish a developmental plan that will provide opportunities for improvement and growth. The human resource review also helps to identify career path moves for high potential employees.

The goal for the customer satisfaction plan, which is currently emerging, is to measure the success of the company from a customer point of view. Bossidy does not want internal quality measures to get in the way of understanding and responding to the customers' perceptions of Allied's products and services. The new approach assumes that Allied needs to look at results from the customers' point of view. The goal is to use the same measures customers would use to measure Allied's performance.

Strengthening Performance Consequences

Over the past five years, Bossidy has sought to align performance with rewards at the individual and group levels. As a result of bringing in about forty people from outside and moving others within the company, about 75 percent of the top 150 managers are now new to their jobs.[17] Bossidy has championed the development of a new reward system that has placed more pay at risk for people at all levels, while giving them the opportunity to make significant gains if the company performs well. The goal in establishing this system was to create a new sense of urgency and higher standards of performance in a culture that had for years tolerated mediocrity (as employees indicated in the firm's opinion surveys). Bossidy pushed for faster decisions on letting go those who could not produce. He also wanted leaders to provide much better performance feedback and coaching for those who remained. In particular, Bossidy wants his leaders to be more direct and helpful in the development of their employees. He has also increased the amount of training received by everyone in the firm in key areas such as total quality management. His view is that everyone suffers if the corporation doesn't have the best people, superbly trained, at all levels.

∽

Making the Goals

To obtain predictable business outcomes in unpredictable markets, organizations must provide individuals and teams with as much autonomy as possible. This autonomy exists amid a complicated web of informal values and formal systems that provide support and guidance. The organizations must have:

- Clear, ambitious performance targets
- Superb execution of initiatives
- Consequences for success and failure on both an individual and organizational level

Organizations must have clear guidelines in place to help ensure that individuals, teams, and the firm as a whole will deliver the expected results. Delivering these results provides a strong foundation for trust. And that foundation is further supported by integrity, which we will discuss in the next chapter.

Achieving Results Survey

Assessing Your Organization or Team

To assess the degree to which your organization or team meets the imperative of achieving results, complete the following survey. The contrasting statements are designed to provoke your thinking regarding the level of performance in your organization and its impact on trust. For each statement, indicate which point along the continuum most accurately describes your organization or team. You can use your ratings to spot areas in need of improvement. The total at the bottom of the page provides a general indication of how well your organization or team is achieving results; the ratings on individual questions provide more detailed feedback. You can also transfer your overall rating in this chapter to Resource One to develop an overall trust profile of your organization or team.

Achieving Results

Assessing Your Organization or Team

In this organization (or team) . . .

People are focused on internal issues and their own personal agendas  Everyone is focused on beating our competition in the marketplace

People are unwilling to set ambitious targets for fear of failure  People are willing to set "stretch" goals and objectives

There is little agreement on our key performance targets and measures  Everyone understands our "vital few" performance targets and measures

We have not executed our business strategies well  We are very good at executing our business strategies

People are interested in the short term and do not focus on building for the future  There is constant work to improve our overall performance capabilities

People often fail to deliver the results they promise  People almost always deliver the results they promise

There is little linkage between performance and rewards and recognition  Rewards and recognition are closely tied to performance

Overall, we have a poor track record of meeting our objectives | 1 | 2 | 3 | 4 | 5 | Overall, we have a superb track record of meeting our objectives

Total Score: _____

Low results: 8–18; Moderate results: 19–29; High results: 30–40

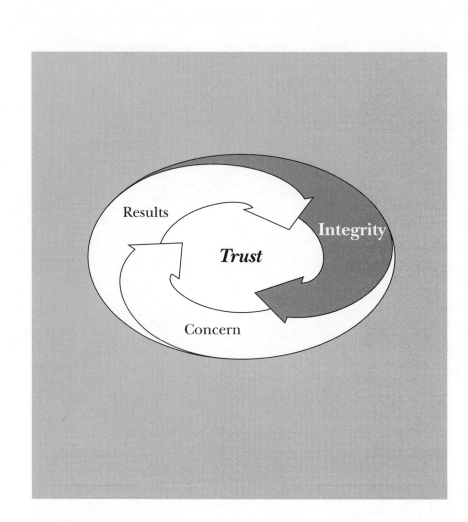

| **Acting with Integrity**

Most of us view integrity as an aspect of honesty. Integrity is adherence to a code of ethics or set of values. It also involves how well our actions match our beliefs. It suggests a wholeness or coherence in our philosophies and values, in our public and private statements, and in our actions across a variety of situations. Integrity is thus a measure of coherence and consistency, and it is key to building and sustaining trust. In sum, we trust those who are honest in what they say and consistent in how they act. We trust those whose behavior is predictable and dependable—even if we disagree with some elements of their actions.

Integrity is a key to explaining how leaders deal with the complex and difficult dilemmas of running large organizations. In their study of leadership effectiveness, Badaracco and Ellsworth found that effective leaders aspired to "consistency and coherence among what they believed, how they managed, and the kinds of organizations they wanted to build."[1] In short, effective leaders strive for consistency in their own behavior and in the actions of their organizations.

Integrity has two meanings in relation to organizational trust:

- First, integrity requires that organizations develop a *set of values and practices* that affirm the rights of customers, associates, and shareholders. This is the "outer core," or conventional notion, of integrity.
- Second, integrity requires that organizations and their leaders develop a *consistent and cohesive approach to business.* Here integrity means that the various parts of the organization, from its values to its work practices, fit together into a coherent approach. This is the "inner core" of integrity, one that is perhaps more important for establishing trust than any other factor.

Inconsistency can suggest that others are either dishonest or are incapable of fulfilling their obligations to us. Doubting the integrity of another is one of the first indicators that trust should be replaced with distrust. This is particularly true with regard to those in leadership positions. To explore both the outer and inner core of integrity, we must examine both the consistencies that are at the heart of integrity and the inconsistencies that are often the root of failures of integrity.

I observed the importance of integrity in a firm that competes in a regulated industry. Increases in this firm's fees needed to be approved by a regulatory board. Over its long history, the firm had become skilled at portraying data and conditions in a way that would increase the likelihood of rate increases. While fraud was not involved, the data seemed to have been slanted in the best interests of the firm. This attitude and behavior affected not only the relationship of the company with the external regulators but leaders in the firm would often conceal or misrepresent data or events when dealing with employees. The result was a well-justified feeling that management could not be trusted.

Consistency as a Form of Integrity

Our expectations influence our assessment of consistency in the behavior of others and have a direct impact on our levels of trust; they also influence the point at which our trust diminishes or is lost. Whether we perceive a certain behavior as supporting or violating our trust depends on what we expect from another in a particular situation. Consistency alone, however, does not necessarily support trust; someone who is consistently incompetent will, of course, not be trusted. But inconsistency between what we expect and what we observe also sparks doubt concerning others' motives.

Most of us become suspicious or distrustful when we perceive inconsistencies in the actions of others or in the actions of the organization at large. These inconsistencies take on particular importance when they have a direct impact on us.

Naturally enough, when inconsistencies surface, people try to understand what is causing them. In many cases, inconsistency suggests that others are motivated by selfish interests; we may conclude, for example, that they are lying to us for personal gain. In other cases, we conclude that inconsistencies are due to simple mistakes—or worse, that people are lying to us to hide their own incompetence. Unless we can discuss the inconsistencies and get to their root, distrust will soon replace any trust that existed.

Several types of consistency are important to the development and maintenance of trust in organizations:

- What we reveal to others reflects what we know
- What we say is aligned with how we behave
- Our behavior is consistent across situations
- Our behavior is consistent over time

Each involves consistency between what we believe, what we say, and how we act.

What Is Revealed? What Is Known?

If we believe that others are sharing the full extent of their knowledge on issues of importance to us, we begin to trust them and their motives. If instead we believe they are not sharing appropriately and that they know more than they are saying, we usually become suspicious.

A positive example of information sharing is found at Procter & Gamble. Each quarter, the firm distributes a video reviewing financial results and key business issues. Group meetings are then held to discuss the information and to bring concerns to the surface. Convex Computer Corporation, a firm with 1,200 employees, provides another example. There the director of manufacturing has regular breakfast meetings with eight to ten employees at a time. This forum gives people in the firm an opportunity to get to know the manufacturing leader better and to ask any questions they might have. In addition, a monthly "focus meeting" is open to anyone in manufacturing and provides an opportunity for people throughout the organization to present ideas or information. These open forums and the direct sharing of critical information and issues involved support a culture of trust.

In many organizations, however, the rumor mill is more helpful as a source of information than official releases from the organization or its leadership. Indeed, a constant theme among employees in many large organizations is "senior leadership is not sharing what we need to know." Consider the reaction of employees who find out about major reorganizations through their local newspapers rather than from their own management teams. In many firms, senior leadership does not want to share the details of an impending change before it has worked through all the details. As a result, rumors become the only source of ongoing information. Employees feel justifiably betrayed if the press picks up the story of a major change and reports it before the organization itself has made an internal announcement.

We distrust those whom we believe are deliberately deceiving us. Whether the deception consists of a subtle manipulation of the truth or a more blatant lie, we distrust because there is no consistency between the words and actions of the person deceiving us.

Alignment Between Words and Actions

Consistency in words and actions is vital if trust is to be sustained. People assess the degree to which others follow through on their statements. They trust those who do what they say they will do and distrust those who do otherwise. At GE, for example, there is a strong emphasis on meeting one's commitments and, in so doing, creating shareholder value. The firm has a culture in which it is stressed that "without leaders who 'walk the talk,' all of our plans, promises and dreams for the future are just that—talk."[2]

Credibility problems are evident in many large organizations. For example, a recent survey at British Telecom found that only one-fifth of its employees thought managers could be relied on to do what they had said they would.[3] Ironically, some organizations and leaders get into trouble because they strive to increase trust by making promises to those they want to influence; in essence, they tell others what those people want to hear in the hope of winning their confidence. But if they then fail to follow through on these promises, they damage their credibility. For example, a CEO may tell members of one of his marketing groups that the company is firmly committed to a new product line. However, the human and financial resources needed to make the product successful are withheld, and finally the CEO pulls all funding for the project and provides no explanation other than to note that the proposed product is no longer commercially viable.

It's easy to see in others: every broken promise, even if due to forces beyond one's control, erodes trust. Earn a reputation as someone who does not follow through on your word, and few will trust you.

Consistency Across Situations

For trust to solidify, words and actions must be consistent across situations. People trust those who are seen as being "straight," sharing the same information with different groups or individuals. This is the case even when the message is not what people want to hear. For example, Continental's CEO, Gordon Bethune, regularly visits the airline's terminals to discuss critical issues with employees. In these meetings, Bethune has been direct to the point of bluntness. For example, he told employees that he would refuse to add a fourth flight attendant because American and Delta don't do it (and Continental could not afford the extra expense). His bluntness was a contrast to the style of past leaders, who would either avoid direct dialogue with employees or put a positive spin on news they thought would be unpopular. His direct and consistent style, regardless of the audience, was instrumental in restoring trust after a decade of what many saw as broken promises and deception.

Suspicion is more likely when people are seen as sharing different information with different groups of people. This is particularly true when the message itself that is being communicated in different settings is contradictory. For example, the senior leadership of a midsize manufacturing firm told a small group of executives on the corporate staff that a thirty–year-old plant in the firm would be closing in order to shift production to a more modern facility. But since leadership was fearful that production would decline if they shared this news with those directly affected, they told hourly employees at the plant site that no decision had been reached. Inevitably, the plant employees heard about the planned closing via the rumor mill long before leadership finally told them—and any trust they had in management was effectively destroyed. The lesson is clear: we distrust those whose words and actions dramatically change with the situation.

A more credible approach would have included a complete disclosure of leadership's concerns and of the factors that would force the closing of a plant or division. In some cases, for example, leaders have told their employees that competitive pressures will force them to close a unit unless it improves productivity, quality, or other key performance measures. The need for improvement is made clear, and sufficient time, resources, and support are provided for developing new work processes. In this situation, the employees of the plant or division are treated as business partners and asked to develop a solution to the problem that both they and the larger corporation are facing. In more extreme cases, employees are told as soon as a decision has been reached that their unit will be closed. They are also told of the transition plan and the support they will be provided.

Consistency over Time

Our perspective changes over time, as it should with changing knowledge and circumstances. Indeed, changes in a firm's strategy are inevitable as markets shift and competition evolves. Ideally, these changes are explained and managed in a way that sustains trust. Microsoft, for example, has shifted its strategy and structure to align with the emergence of the Internet. This significant change was positioned as a competitive necessity that offered new opportunities if aggressively pursued. Microsoft did not want to fall victim to the arrogance and complacency found in many dominant firms.

But frequent and abrupt shifts in position will undermine trust. This is particularly true when those observing the change don't understand why the management's words or actions have shifted. Some organizations, such as Unisys, have undergone four or five changes in business strategy and organization over a ten-year interval. Credibility has eroded as the competitive positioning of the firm has changed from one year to the next. In other cases, commitments made several years ago must often be altered when conditions require a new approach. For example, when AT&T split into a long-distance parent and seven regional offspring in 1984, senior leadership told employees that the split would not jeopardize their jobs. At the time, AT&T employed almost one million people. By early 1996, 250,000 people had been dropped from the payrolls, and AT&T has announced another round of layoffs that will eliminate 30,000 or more jobs. While AT&T has certainly attempted to demonstrate the need for smaller payroll, many within the firm still remember the initial promise. They also remember the mistakes made by leadership that have resulted in less growth than might have been expected.

Another example is found in the decision to relocate the corporate headquarters of London Fog. Several years ago, the new CEO announced a move of the headquarters from Eldersburg, Maryland, to Darien, Connecticut (just twenty minutes from his home). Eighteen months later, the CEO departed and his replacement announced a move back to Eldersburg. Not only was the firm shifting from one position to another, it was making decisions based on what appeared to be the personal interests of its leaders.[4]

The level of distrust within many large firms can be traced to the failure of leadership to provide a coherent sense of direction. Distrust is likely when leaders keep changing their story about their firm's strategic direction and the source of failures in the marketplace. Imagine, for example, that a CEO tells financial analysts in September that his firm's business strategy will not change and that the organization will "stay the course." In January, he announces that a sudden decline in market share has forced the development of a new strategic plan and organizational structure. The plan that he supported "1000 percent" several months earlier is completely abandoned. Where is the trust? Is it any wonder that after yet another strategy is introduced—with no admission that early efforts were flawed—this plan fails as well?

Understanding Expectations

As these failures of integrity show us, trust is based in part on being able to predict the behavior of others. Consistency between what we expect and how others behave is one important basis for trust. Thus, those seeking to build trust must always consider people's expectations in seeking to understand the impact of their decisions. Gaps between people's expectations and what people observe will result in distrust. For example, an employee in an organization undergoing a downsizing notes, "I've worked hard and I'm entitled to expect a reasonable degree of security and a reasonable chance at promotion. I'm cynical because the company expects us to keep giving, but it doesn't give in return." The downsizing brought the employee's assumptions about job security to the surface. Since reality did not meet his expectations, his distrust of the organization and its leaders came to the fore. Could this loss of trust have been prevented? Can it be healed?

Organizations and their leaders cannot simply strive to fulfill all the expectations—reasonable or not—of employees or associates. But an important leadership role is to create an environment in which expectations are understood, shared, and generally met. In other words, expectations must be met—or revised so that they can be met—if trust is to be sustained.

These dilemmas are suggestive of the larger issue of organizational credibility. Several recent surveys, for instance, found that a majority of those polled in seventy companies didn't believe what management said or that they were well informed of their company's plans.[5] How can trust be sustained when a majority of people are suspicious about what they are being told by the organization and its leaders?

Building Organizational Integrity

Integrity and the trust that derives from it are based on a few essential actions:

* *Define a clear purpose.* Articulate and reinforce over time a clear strategic vision, performance targets, and a set of operating principles for the organization.

* *Confront reality.* Be open to sharing and receiving essential information related to the current and probable future status of your business.

* *Have open agendas.* Deal with others in a straightforward manner that reveals the true motives and desired outcomes.

* *Follow through.* Honor commitments; when this is not possible, explain the reasons to those affected. Reward those who meet their commitments. Deal in a tough but equitable and predictable manner with those who do not.

Defining a Clear Purpose

Organizations and their leaders are well served by articulating and consistently reinforcing over time a clear strategic vision and set of operating principles. The presence of these "guiding principles" helps build trust because people know what is most important and how they will be judged. Consequently, expectations among people in different areas and at different levels are more likely to be in line. There are fewer misunderstandings, and this strengthens trust.

To be effective in building trust, these guiding principles, the organization's stated values, must be supported by reinforcing actions. As we've seen, discrepancies between what is espoused and what is done are among the fundamental causes of distrust. Two types of consistency with respect to purpose and values are particularly important: consistency around strategic priorities and consistency around core operating values.

Key Strategic Priorities

The articulation of a few key strategic priorities is essential to create an environment where the goals are clearly understood. In short, people need to understand what is most important as they go about making decisions in their jobs. Expectations around the organization's primary purpose must be aligned if people are to be given autonomy.

These priorities may involve the primary goal of the organization or the primary strategies used to achieve that goal. Examples of a primary goal include maximizing shareholder value, meeting customer requirements, and producing innovative products. The primary goal of the organization, of course, is balanced by other objectives, but there must be a clear single objective on which the others rest.

Throughout his leadership tenure, Roberto Goizueta, CEO of Coca-Cola, has emphasized the need to create shareholder wealth. He has adjusted the firm's goals and management practices to align with this larger objective. He has also established a set of practices and symbols that remind members of the organization that shareholder wealth is their primary objective. For example, a video monitor at the entrance of Coca-Cola headquarters shows the firm's stock price, which is updated several times a day. This reminder is the first thing employees see as they walk into the building each morning and the last thing they see when they go home at the end of the day.

In a high-trust culture, organizational members also need to know what primary strategies to keep in mind as they perform their jobs. For example, in some firms customer satisfaction is seen as the primary means of achieving financial results. Other firms view product innovation as the key to long-term growth and profitability. Whatever the specifics, consistency and follow-through (in contrast to a rotating set of priorities with little long-term commitment) are key to supporting trust.

Jack Welch is a prime example of consistency in action. His behavior since becoming General Electric's CEO was described by Steve Kerr, vice president of corporate management development:

> Welch has been amazing in the degree of consistency he has shown around his core beliefs. You can go back to the first speech he made at Harvard in 1981 and see the same themes that he focuses on today (such as the need for productivity growth). He changes his metaphors, but the basic themes and his overall approach have not changed over time. His consistency over time is one of the reasons he engenders a great deal of trust. You may not always agree with what he says, but you damn well know what he stands for.

In many respects, Welch's legacy may be his tenacity in articulating and staying with a few core themes over his years as the leader of one of the most important companies in the world.

Core Operating Values
Consistency around core operating values is also critical; these values should clarify how the organization operates in striving to achieve its objectives. Expectations around how members behave are, after all, as important as expectations around what we are seeking to accomplish.

Hewlett-Packard is one of the best known examples of a firm that places great emphasis on operating values. Over its history, the firm has reinforced a particular set of values, described as the HP Way. Pete Peterson, senior vice president of personnel, explained it as follows:

Over the years at HP, we have had influential leaders who lived our values. Bill and Dave, our founders, created a set of principles on how we run HP. Their own behavior set an example of what we value as a firm and how we operate. For example, they believed that people want to do a good job and must be trusted to do what is necessary for HP to be successful. In all of their interactions, they demonstrated this belief in the ability of people to contribute. Today, we have new leaders but the themes are the same. We are building on the legacy created by the founders. Our current CEO, Lew Platt, is very open to employees in the organization. I know it is a small thing, but he never fails to return a phone call. His responsiveness signals that he cares and wants to support us in whatever way he can.

Confronting Reality

Trust requires the achievement of results. This cannot occur without knowledge about the organization, about the success of its products and services, and about the capabilities of organizational members. Integrity involves full disclosure of important information and a willingness to deal with tough issues. Integrity requires a willingness to deal with the reality of an organization's current competitive situation and the likelihood of success in the future. Confronting reality means seeing the world the way it is and not the way you may wish or hope it would be. In particular, integrity demands honesty in assessing the performance of an organization and its members and the likelihood of future improvements. This requires a level of honesty rare in most corporations. Consider Steve Kerr's observation regarding the need for honesty in a high-trust culture:

> Sometimes we fail, but we know what is needed—namely, an open approach to dealing with reality and a can-do attitude to fixing what is broken. Welch wants people to deal with reality and address the tough issues we face. In the past, people were more intent on looking good, even if it meant hiding their problems.

Honestly confronting reality has been one of Welch's strong points, yet his reputation for getting results often takes the limelight. Before anyone else did, he saw the need to improve corporations' productivity dramatically. In the early 1980s, when GE's profits were robust, Welch took the painful path and confronted the looming reality of a highly competitive global economy.

Having Open Agendas

Beyond a willingness to deal with reality, integrity also requires openness about one's objectives and motives in a particular situation. In a high-trust culture, what you see is what you get. In a low-trust culture, people hide their true objectives and, in doing so, mislead others. Low-trust organizations are rife with "hidden agendas" and complicated political positionings. In contrast, one of the attributes of a high-trust culture is a minimum amount of political behavior and an overall sense that people are dealing with issues in an up-front way.

Pepsi, which has a reputation for having a results-driven culture, also emphasizes the importance of integrity. As its CEO, Craig Weatherup, has said, "I have found that people do business with those they trust—which is based in large part on integrity." And he understands integrity's link to openness: "As a leader, I want people to be open and honest about the facts. I also want them to be fair and consistent in how they look at issues. Those are the people you trust and want as members of your organization."[6]

A high-trust culture requires that people be up front about their intent and the facts as they know them. It is particularly important to balance the need to encourage openness with the need to establish consequences based on performance. Penalizing in the name of performance management people who deliver bad news, for example, will result in less candor about the problems facing an organization or team. While holding people accountable for results is imperative, leadership that creates a culture of harsh consequences for any bad news will ultimately shut off communication.

Also important to openness and ultimately to integrity is the degree to which people will manipulate others in order to achieve their objectives. Weatherup voices a common sentiment in saying, "I begin to distrust people when I sense they are manipulating me or others toward some personal gain or to make a bad situation look better than it is. Once I feel that someone is so inclined, it is very hard for me to trust them and work with them. There is no neutral category—that is, I either trust them or I don't." Even the best of results will not last if people feel that they have been manipulated in the process. As Weatherup says, "people will block you at every turn if they think you are a phony or have deceived them in some way."

Following Through

Acting with integrity means that we keep our promises, both explicit and implicit, and follow through on commitments. Integrity demands that when, for whatever reason, we cannot meet the commitments we have made, we are honest about it. Integrity demands that firms and their leaders treat people fairly in recognizing and rewarding them for performance. In contrast, failing to give credit where credit is due or failing to be objective in performance appraisals can create a great deal of distrust. Craig Weatherup of Pepsi speaks to the need for fairness in sustaining trust:

> Some people see Pepsi as a tough place to work. We have a reputation for being an "up or out" organization. The reality, however, is that we value candor and directness in telling people where they stand. There is no ambiguity around performance at Pepsi, which some people perceive as harsh. I see it as an important and necessary part of how we operate. You can't create a high-trust culture unless people perform. Building capability requires very direct feedback and, as appropriate, consequences for performance. We are tough but we are also fair.

Senior leaders erode their credibility when they make commitments and fail to deliver. Then, to compound their mistakes, some act as if they never made the commitment. As Richard Simonds, a Hewlett-Packard project manager, explained:

> At HP, we do what we say we will do for our customers—whatever it takes. This causes a great deal of stress in the organization, but it is our firm's reputation on the line. We value the trust we have earned and will do everything we can to meet or exceed our promises to our customers. Thus, people expect others within the company to meet their commitments to each other—otherwise, we can't possibly meet our customer commitments. In this company, you are expected to follow through on what you promise others.

As part of meeting commitments, there is an expectation in most organizations that people will be rewarded based on their contributions over a sustained period of time. Steve Kerr of GE speaks to this expectation:

> The senior leader has to assess the performance of his key executives against stretch targets while still giving them the room to fail as they take risks for the benefit of the company. A critical aspect of trust is how you handle mistakes as an organization. Welch, for example, can be very hard on people. But with Welch, mistakes are not fatal. He will listen to data and revise his opinion of someone if the facts suggest otherwise.

Following through with fairness, then, does not mean being soft or overly forgiving. The need to achieve results means that firms are direct in dealing with performance issues at the organizational, team, and individual levels.

Acting with Integrity at Motorola

Integrity involves adherence to a set of ethical and fair practices as well as a consistent and cohesive approach to one's business. These levels, the outer and inner core of integrity, are well illustrated in the actions of Motorola over its history.

Integrity's Outer Core

Motorola has one of the most respected approaches to ethical business practices in the world. The company's leadership has made it very clear that violating one of the firm's standards of ethics in the conduct of business, which is applied uniformly around the world, will result in immediate dismissal. Robert Galvin, the founder's son who transformed the firm during his years as CEO, tells a story that reflects the Motorola code of ethics:

> The year was 1950 and Motorola was doing less than $200 million in annual business (compared to $20 billion today). The firm had placed a $10 million bid for a project with a South American government for a microwave communication system. At year's end,

Motorola won the contract. But the manager in charge of the project told Galvin that they were not going to take the order. Puzzled, Galvin asked why. He was told that those buying the equipment wanted Motorola to rewrite the bid for $11 million, with a justification for more training. He added, "We know where that extra million will go—into the pockets of some of those generals. We told them we would not take the order." Galvin thanked his manager for doing the right thing, even though every employee in the company would suffer by at least $100 in his or her profit-sharing check as a result of the lost order. He also noted that Motorola would not take the bid even if the generals had backed down and come back with the bid of $10 million. He pointed out that Motorola's integrity would be questioned if they conducted business with those known to engage in unethical business practices. The cost to the firm would be much greater than the $10 million in lost revenue.[7]

Integrity is often viewed in relation to how a firm acts in relation to external stakeholders such as customers, suppliers, and alliance partners. The impact of such behavior, however, is closely linked to how employees are treated and how they treat each other. A firm that engages in unethical business practices with customers is likely to engage in questionable practices with its employees. In other words, a willingness to violate standards of ethics permeates a culture. The result is an erosion of integrity throughout a company. In such cases, trust is elusive at best.

Integrity's Inner Core

Motorola also is exemplary with regard to the inner core of integrity, which I define as coherence and consistency in a firm's business approach. The company's approach to quality over the past fifteen years provides a notable example of organizational consistency and coherence.

In the late 1970s, Robert Galvin found himself at the helm of a successful firm founded by his father in 1928 to sell car radios. He called a historic meeting of his top seventy-five executives to celebrate the firm's successes and chart the direction for the future. But toward the end of a session in which the financial people reviewed a series of positive financial reports, the executive who was responsible for the best division in the company stood up and said, "Our quality levels really stink." This direct criticism was taken seriously, as Motorola had throughout its history abandoned products such as television tubes when it could no longer compete. The comment was also consistent with what is described as Motorola's "cult of dissent." Surprised and somewhat chastened, Galvin and his team began studying factories at other companies around the globe. They found that the quality standards at these other factories were higher; in fact, the Japanese had quality standards that were, in some cases, a thousand times higher than Motorola's.

Galvin returned to corporate headquarters and asked for a tenfold quality improvement. The leadership team established standards and measured current performance. They put the new targets into place and held managers accountable for improvement. Over time, Galvin's quality champions advocated a much more aggressive target, which they called Six Sigma (nearly perfect quality performance). A decision was made to move forward quickly—but with a view toward long-term improvement and profitability. The road to perfection would take decades.

The introduction of Six Sigma was broad and deep. Galvin and his team preached the benefits of the program at every opportunity—both within Motorola and to external audiences. This "top-down commitment" touched every Motorola office and employee. All employees were given training, and Motorola became one of the highest-spending firms in terms of education (over $100 million per year). New employees were told that they had to meet specific quality requirements or risk losing their jobs. Quality issues were moved from last to first on leadership agendas. Over time, most performance incentives were linked to quality requirements. Suppliers, such as IBM, were even told to apply for the Baldridge Quality Award or lose Motorola as a customer. Fifteen years after launching its quality program, Motorola is still the single best model on how to use quality to revitalize a company.[8]

The relentless path to Six Sigma reflected Galvin's view that leaders must follow through on their commitments. Galvin anticipated the increasing importance of quality in his industry and fully committed himself and his firm to its realization. Reflecting on his successes, he notes, "People ask me how I've had the interest and the zeal to hang in there and do what I've done. I say, 'Because my father treated me with very stern discipline. He trusted me.' I'm stuck, I've got to see the trust through. He trusted me. I trust other people. And they did the job. All I've been is an instrument to see that what got started is carried on."[9]

The Six Sigma story at Motorola demonstrates the importance of integrity in sustaining people's trust. Compare the Motorola story with the large majority of firms that try one program after another, abandoning an approach as soon as hard choices or significant investments are required. In these firms, employees often resist new efforts because they believe these efforts will eventually be abandoned. They are also likely to question whether management has a coherent philosophy and approach to making the business grow. Motorola, in contrast, aligned its practices to reinforce its commitment over the long term. It also linked its various initiatives into an integrated agenda for change. Thus, the firm acts with integrity in sustaining over time a few core initiatives that are enacted in a coherent way.

∽

Practicing Principles and Values

Integrity, the degree of coherence or consistency between words and actions, is a key imperative for building and sustaining trust. It does not simply consist of rigid adherence to a set of prescriptions. Instead, it is the degree to which individuals, teams, and organizations fully embody the values they hold to be most important.

Most of the organizations that have built higher levels of trust have done so as a result of a strong leader or leadership team that follows through with a well-known game plan. These organizations have also built management processes that ensure follow-through and discipline during implementation of new initiatives. GE and Hewlett-Packard serve as examples of consistency in how they have stressed the fundamentals of their business philosophy. Welch has varied very little from the vision he articulated soon after becoming CEO in the early 1980s; the basic principles are still in effect today. Similarly, Hewlett-Packard's founders put into place a set of business principles and values that have changed very little over the past five decades—even as Hewlett-Packard's products and services have changed considerably.

In contrast, trust is most difficult to sustain in environments where the leadership team is constantly changing its direction or values. In these groups, people are unsure what leadership and the firm in general stand for. Continuity over time is critical in building faith that the organization or team is acting with integrity (that is, consistently adhering to a well-known set of values and principles). Ineffective leaders do whatever the last person they spoke to recommended, or they plunge ahead with the latest good idea that captures their imagination. To trust their leaders, followers have to know what those leaders stand for and how they will behave over time.

To demonstrate integrity, then, we must

- Define a clear purpose
- Confront reality
- Have open agendas
- Follow through

Often heard phrases such as "dealing with reality," "saying what you believe," and "walking the talk" reflect these principles and underscore the need for consistency within organizations.

Whether these principles are practiced or violated, whether the outer and inner core of integrity remain firm, has a direct impact on trust. If an organization's strategic focus and business priorities constantly change, it will never earn the trust of those who work either within the organization or with it. Leaders should take note: they too must keep their strategic focus and business priorities steady in order to be trusted. When organizations and their leaders seek results at any cost, the trust they need for long-term financial performance will be eroded.

Integrity is the basis of all long-term business relationships. Together with achieving results, it is further supported by demonstrations of caring, discussed in the following chapter.

Acting with Integrity Survey

Assessing Your Organization or Team

To assess the degree to which your organization or team meets the imperative of acting with integrity, complete the following survey. The contrasting statements are designed to provoke your thinking regarding the level of performance in your organization and its impact on trust. For each statement, indicate which point along the continuum most accurately describes your organization or team. You can use your ratings to spot areas in need of improvement. The total at the bottom of the page provides a general indication of integrity in your organization or team, while the ratings on individual questions provide more detailed feedback. You can also transfer your overall rating in this chapter to Resource One to develop an overall trust profile of your organization or team.

Acting with Integrity

Assessing Your Organization or Team

In this organization (or team) . . .

We are constantly
changing our strategic
direction and priorities

We have a coherent
strategic vision and
clear set of priorities

Leaders say one thing
and do another when
it comes to our
principles and values

Leaders "walk the talk"
with regard to our
principles and values

The grapevine is more
reliable than what we
hear from leadership
You can believe what
you hear from those in
leadership positions

People either deny or
put a positive "spin" on
negative information
People deal openly
with facts even when
they are negative

Problems are dealt with
in a way that leaves
people feeling abused

People are treated
fairly in resolving
problems or dealing
with adversity

Promises and
commitments are
broken all the time
People follow through
with their promises
and commitments

People think first
about what is best
for themselves and
then the firm

People do what is
"right" for the firm
even if it is at some
expense to themselves

Overall, there is a
low level of integrity
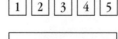
Overall, there is a
high level of integrity

Total Score: _____

Low integrity: 8–18; Moderate integrity: 19–29; High integrity: 30–40

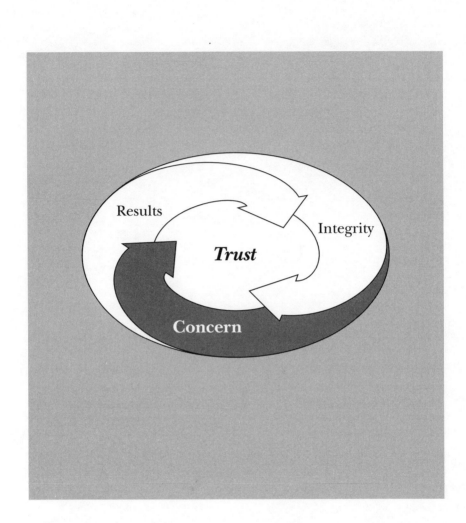

Chapter Five

Demonstrating Concern

In the previous two chapters, we explored the relationship between trust and an organization's ability to achieve results and act with integrity. A third and equally important imperative for building trust is demonstrating concern for others. At the most basic level, we assume that those we trust will not deliberately take advantage of us. In other words, trust requires that those in whom we place our faith remain responsive to our needs, even in the face of potentially conflicting pressures. Trust, therefore, requires that we go beyond results and integrity: we must also show that we understand and are responsive to the needs of others.

The type of concern that trust requires is reflected in the ideas and practices of Hewlett-Packard. In his autobiography, David Packard discussed the case of a Hewlett-Packard employee who in the late 1940s, developed tuberculosis and had to take a two-year leave of absence. The company provided some financial help to the employee's family. They then took the next step and developed a plan to protect employees and their families in the future: Hewlett-Packard established a program of catastrophic medical insurance at a time when this type of coverage was virtually unknown.[1]

Demonstrating concern, however, is becoming more difficult as the pressure for profit becomes more intense. The tension between profits and people, bottom-line results and human considerations, presents a difficult dilemma that is becoming more pronounced—as it must in an environment that demands profit in increasingly competitive markets. The significant and widespread downsizings we have witnessed over the past decade in corporate America have had an enormous impact. And the layoffs continue at a rapid pace—even in apparently healthy firms.

All of these changes have eroded the sense of leadership concern and employee trust. As one midlevel employee in a large firm commented to me, "there is a general feeling among the employees that the company no longer cares for them. Broken is the unspoken bond of trust which said you care deeply for me and I'll care deeply for you."

The expectations of various groups are in flux. For example, some employees believe that their organizations should provide lifetime job security. Others believe their organizations cannot guarantee lifetime employment but are obligated to provide equal opportunity for advancement and development. Still others believe that organizations should show an active interest in the careers of their people and assume responsibility for making each employee successful. Some expect leaders to take a personal interest in their lives, including family issues and concerns. Expectations vary widely, and each has an impact on trust. As a result, those who wish to be trusted must understand others' expectations. Clearly, they cannot meet everyone's varied demands and expectations. But they can—and to be successful, they must—work to gain a common set of assumptions about the rights and duties of organizational members at all levels.

Expectations relative to corporate concern are changing—sometimes painfully. In the past, many organizations operated in a paternalistic manner. Employees were assured lifetime security in return for loyalty and, in some cases, conformity to rigid rules. Over the past decade, most corporations have altered their policies, and fewer firms now guarantee lifetime employment or promotions based on seniority. In many companies, demonstrating concern now revolves around offering opportunity rather than providing security. These organizations provide ample opportunity to grow on the job and in one's career—but they do not guarantee job security in the absence of individual and organizational performance.

Once again, an organization's demonstrations of concern are perhaps best illustrated in such firms as Hewlett-Packard. David Packard believes that the essence of HP's culture is sharing the risks and rewards of making a business grow. Paternalism is therefore replaced with both the positives and the negatives of joint ownership. Packard writes that at the core of HP's practices is the notion of sharing: "sharing the responsibilities for defining and meeting goals, sharing in company ownership through stock purchase plans, sharing in profits, sharing the opportunities for personal and professional development, and even sharing the burdens created by occasional downturns in business."[2]

The 1990s will see the demise of paternalism in most of our largest firms. This does not mean, however, that corporations will become ruthless places where only the self-serving survive. The new contract between organizations and their members, which is being developed in firms such as IBM and Levi Strauss, will have a clear performance mandate. There is no choice. Yet the best firms will also be places in which people will want to work and will feel supported by people at all levels.

Demonstrating Concern for Others

Concern and the trust that derives from it are based on a few essential actions:

* *Build one vision, one company.* Develop an identity and esprit de corps in the larger organization that counterbalances individual, team, and unit perspectives.

* *Show confidence in people's ability.* Believe that members of the organization have the necessary motivation and ability to deliver on the corporation's business objectives. Provide support to organizational members in relation to their need and consistent with a larger set of values regarding the value of people.

* *Establish familiarity and dialogue.* Establish formal and informal processes to ensure that people have sufficient contact with each other and an understanding of each others' perspectives.

* *Recognize contributions.* Create organizational approaches to recognize and reward the contributions of people in different groups and roles.

Each of these actions plays a critical role in demonstrating concern, as the following sections describe.

Building One Vision, One Company

Demonstrating concern begins with the establishment of a larger sense of identity that transcends individual and team points of view.

In high-trust settings, the identity of the larger organization becomes highly visible and is, in part, internalized by its members. At Hewlett-Packard, for example, there is a feeling that everyone works for one firm, despite the existence of relatively autonomous divisions. Moreover, most employees believe that Hewlett-Packard—given its history, its values, and its technical and financial successes—is unique and worthy of their respect and support. The goal is to align practices so that what is good for the firm and what is good for individuals are not in opposition but in close accord. At Hewlett-Packard, the potential split between what is good for the individual and what is good for the company is less pronounced than in most organizations.

A "one vision, one company" mind-set in which shared identification is maximized and distinctions among individuals and groups are minimized can be achieved through a variety of mechanisms. One approach is to minimize hierarchical and status distinctions among levels in the organization. At Intel, for example, CEO Andrew Grove, one of the wealthiest people in America, works in a cubicle rather than a private office. He and his fellow executives fly coach class and rent subcompact cars (as do all other Intel employees).[3] Hewlett-Packard provides an even more powerful illustration of reducing or eliminating status barriers. The characteristics of its culture contribute to "one vision, one company" through the following means:

- *Limited Hierarchy.* HP has 112,000 employees and only 32 vice presidents. There is a hierarchy, but it is much less dominant and evident than in many other organizations.
- *Few Status Symbols.* HP downplays symbols of status. For example, the physical work environment is designed to minimize differences among employee levels. Everyone works in a cubicle of some type, although some may be a bit larger than others. There are no executive dining rooms, no fancy offices, and no reserved parking spaces.
- *Informality.* Since the start, HP has had an informal culture. For example, everyone called the founders by their first names. According to Pete Peterson, senior vice president of personnel, Hewlett would tell those who called him Mr. Hewlett that "Mr. Hewlett is my father's name. My name is Bill."

An opposite culture, with an emphasis on hierarchy, status symbols, and formality, has distinctions that serve to undermine the "one company" concept and increase the likelihood of suspicion. In addition, a firm might have supportive human resources practices but no overarching sense of corporate identity. As a consultant, I have worked with a number of firms where people focus primarily on their own needs and the needs of their local business units or teams. Consequently, the level of distrust among groups is often high.

Showing Confidence in People's Ability

A cohesive vision is a start, but more is needed to ensure high levels of trust. Even employment security, fair compensation, and few layoffs cannot ensure it. Leaders must also show their faith in people.

Throughout its history, HP has consistently put into place organizational structures and processes that reflect its founders' confidence in people. Hewlett and Packard wanted to build an organization that was quite different from the firms that populated the American landscape in the late thirties and forties. In particular, they wanted to move away from what they described as a military model based on rigid control and discipline to create a firm that was the kind of place where they would want to work. More than any corporation with which I am familiar, HP has developed a cohesive and integrated approach to trusting its people.

This sentiment is reflected in the first of Hewlett-Packard's values, which proclaims, "We have trust and respect for individuals. We approach each situation with the understanding that people want to do a good job and will do so, given the proper tools and support. We attract highly capable, innovative people and recognize their efforts and contributions to the company. HP people can contribute enthusiastically and share in the success that they make possible."[4]

This value is reiterated by Bill Hewlett in a later Hewlett-Packard publication: "I think in general terms that [the HP Way] is policies and actions that flow from the belief that men and women want to do a good job, a creative job, and that if they are provided the proper environment they will do so. But that's only part of it. Closely coupled with this is the HP tradition of treating each individual with consideration and respect, and recognizing individual achievements."[5]

As Pete Peterson summarized, "there are a number of practices that reflect our belief in people and the need for trust. Early in the firm's existence, we did away with time clocks and trusted people to manage their own time. This approach was quite radical in the 1940s when many people were paid by the hour. Similarly, we put into place flexible time ahead of other large corporations. We did this because our people benefited from having flexibility in when they came into work. We trusted that they would meet their time and work commitments. These are but two examples of how we have aligned our human resource practices with our high-trust culture."

Almost every company has some statement of values that expresses the importance of its employees and the willingness of the firm to empower them. What sets HP apart is the fact that the firm's long-standing commitment to people was a personal value of its founders that has been put into practice at every level. Those who work for HP are the first to admit that the HP Way is an ideal that they sometimes fail to reach; they do, however, continue to strive for that ideal. In contrast, leaders in many other firms still believe that people are either motivated by selfish interests or unable to fulfill their business objectives unless closely supervised.

It is true that the relationship between financial and human considerations has never been easy. While it is common to hear in most corporations that "people are our greatest asset," the perception of how firms manage their people is often quite different. A *Newsweek* magazine cover, for example, calls the leaders of some our largest firms "Corporate Killers"—with accompanying photographs of those who have significantly reduced their workforce. The caption beneath the headline reads, "Wall Street loves layoffs. But the public is scared as hell."[6]

Over the past decade, the leader in putting into motion the corporate restructuring trend has been Jack Welch. He started what has now become common practice in most industries— namely, significantly improving productivity, in part through reductions in workforce. The balance is not easy and is one that Welch has struggled with. Steve Kerr, vice president of corporate management development at GE, notes:

Jack believes that we must be hardheaded but softhearted. Hardheaded is making the tough business calls that are required in order for us to remain competitive. This might, for example, require that we fire someone who is incapable of doing his or her job, or reduce the size of our workforce in order to reduce our costs. The softhearted part involves the way we go about the hard-headed decisions, such as how we support our people during periods of downsizing. We were ahead of the curve in restructuring our businesses and thus took some heat for the tough calls we made. But if you look at how we handled the changes, I think you would agree that we acted as fairly and compassionately as possible. GE pioneered new layoff benefits, put in the first approach to early notification, and broke all the ground rules for generous severance. We went the extra mile—although I'm not minimizing the pain that was caused all the way around.[7]

Support, of course, is more than managing downsizings in a way that attempts to mitigate the pain they cause. On a day-to-day basis, firms can provide support, particularly in being flexible about meeting employee needs. Consider, for example, the actions taken by U.S. West when the child of one of its employees was recently diagnosed with cancer. The employee wanted to be near her daughter rather than commute 250 miles back and forth to the hospital—and U.S. West found her a temporary position in the city where her daughter was hospitalized. Innovative firms like U.S. West believe that support and, in particular, flexibility are competitive issues, resulting in higher productivity and commitment to the firm.

Other firms, such as DuPont, are well known for their focus on supporting employees in a variety of ways to make the balance between work and life demands more manageable. DuPont started its work/life program in 1985 and made it as a mainstream issue in order to enhance both employee commitment and business results. Through this program, DuPont has instituted generous leave policies, flexible work options, subsidized and emergency child and elder care, dependent care reimbursement for business travel, and a dependent care spending account. A recent ten-year study of the business impact of these programs indicates that employees who feel more supported by the company are more committed to their work and to DuPont.[8]

Duke Power provides another example of how a company can demonstrate concern. On consolidating its ninety-eight local customer service offices several years ago, Duke wanted to improve service and cut costs. The manager in charge of the reorganization realized that improvement was contingent on providing employees with the flexibility to manage better the various pressures in their lives. The new facility built a child care center in alliance with other large firms such as Allstate and IBM. Rotating swing shifts, which employees disliked, were eliminated, and people were allowed to bid, on the basis of seniority, on stable schedules. Employees were also given more privileges, including the right to change shifts among themselves without approval from a supervisor. In sum, a host of changes designed to give employees more support has resulted in a leaner, more flexible organization with much lower attrition rates.[9]

Establishing Familiarity and Dialogue

It is difficult to demonstrate concern for those you don't know. Therefore, trust requires familiarity, being available and approachable to all members of the organization. Familiarity means listening to others and understanding their point of view. It also involves, as appropriate, spending social time with people and taking an active interest in their work and careers.

Many firms have developed ways to ensure that their people have sufficient contact with each other. HP, for example, is widely recognized for its emphasis on "management by walking around," but it also has a host of other less well known means of keeping people in constant contact. At HP, there is a requirement that leaders work in open offices located near their employees; an open-door policy facilitates contact across levels; frequent team and company social gatherings, cross-division quarterly meetings, and regular town-hall sessions between the senior leadership and divisional employees help ensure communication.

In many other corporations, however, people at different levels and in different groups are isolated from each other. A variety of informal and formal mechanisms keep people from having direct and ongoing contact with each other. Unfortunately, in the absence of familiarity, people can easily misinterpret the actions of others—

particularly those in leadership positions. The results are often increased suspicion and negative assumptions about others' motives.

A common employee point of view might be voiced as follows: "I get upset because we want communications and instead we get propaganda. That is not communications. Communications is asking people what their problems are and what they can do to help. Management needs to ask the lower-level employees what is going on with them." From the employee's perspective, neither their needs nor expectations are met when leadership (either of the organization as a whole or of the functional groups) simply announces a new policy or sets directives from afar.

On the other hand, a number of basic actions, both formal and informal, can increase familiarity. These might include locating different levels and groups near each other, instead of in separate facilities; holding off-site meetings to address critical business issues; conducting joint training and socialization of new employees; hosting both small and large informal social events; establishing joint projects or task forces; setting up shared customer visits; instituting regular town-hall meetings; conducting "no-agenda" visits with others in their work sites; and using e-mail postings for speedy communication. Each firm needs to develop a culturally appropriate way of building familiarity over time.

Ultimately, however, the answer to developing familiarity goes deeper than a set of organizational techniques. For example, Greg Brenneman, COO of Continental, makes a point of visiting informally with employees at every level when he travels to the firm's field operations. He will also leave his corporate office and talk with headquarters staff to get a sense of how they are doing on their jobs. In our interview, Brenneman admitted that unlike many senior executives he has seen, he likes spending time with people and will take every opportunity to do so. He looks for ways to interact with employees around issues of importance to their business.

Recognizing Contributions

In part, concern for others means that they are fairly compensated for their performance and, in a broader sense, recognized for the contribution they make to the larger organization. As Fukuyama, a noted social observer writes, "all human beings believe they have a certain inherent worth or dignity. When that worth is not recognized adequately by others, they feel anger; when they don't live up to others' evaluation, they feel shame; and when they are evaluated appropriately, they feel pride. The desire for recognition is an extraordinarily powerful part of the human psyche."[10]

In keeping with the HP Way, Hewlett-Packard has developed approaches to recognizing individual and team contributions. Based on the founders' "strong belief that individuals be treated with consideration and respect and that their achievements be recognized," those at HP have worked hard "to create an environment in which people have a chance to be their best, to realize their potential, and to be recognized for their achievements."[11] Each HP division develops its own reward and recognition program that may involve cash bonuses, time off, team celebrations, special awards or ceremonies, and stock options. More important, the firm has developed an informal culture that takes pride in the accomplishments of its people and responds with both formal and informal efforts.

Other companies have also developed recognition-rich cultures. At Southwest Airlines, building a strong sense of commitment to the firm is an important part of the culture. Southwest employees are well paid compared with their counterparts at other airlines. Celebrations—from spontaneous "fun sessions," to Christmas parties beginning in September, to a lavish annual awards banquet where individual and team contributions to the whole are glorified—are an important part of the work environment.[12] Levi Strauss engages in a number of practices to reinforce performance-related recognition. At its headquarters, employees give "You Are Great" certificates to colleagues whom they believe have done a superb job. The certificates can be used for gifts or kept as a sign of appreciation. In addition, department heads are given a fund out of which they can give immediate financial rewards to those doing an outstanding job. The firm's divisions also hold formal events where outstanding performers are given "personal hero" awards.[13]

These types of rewards and recognition must be carefully crafted so that competition for them does not result in more conflict or suspicion among people. At the least, teams (versus individuals) should be recognized whenever appropriate. In addition, rewards should be offered to everyone in the organization when performance warrants collective recognition.

In fact, most high-trust organizations have developed approaches to sharing among all levels the profits generated when their business meets or exceeds its targets. These programs often involve profit sharing for the firm as a whole, stock investment programs that subsidize widespread ownership, and stock option programs that reward people who contribute to the organization over the long term. An approach that involves most if not all the members of the firm is particularly important in an age when the compensation of senior executives has skyrocketed.

Some firms have stock programs that are available to every member of the organization; more are developing such programs. Chase Bank, for example, is making stock options available to all employees who in the process are being given training in the firm's business fundamentals and financial performance.[14] Back in the late 1980s, Pepsi wanted to develop a program that would encourage people to think and act like owners—and that would reward them as such. The program that the HR group developed, Pepsi's "Share-Power" program, nurtures an ownership culture within one of the largest firms in the world. Through it, the company offers stock to all full-time employees based on their salary. The options, offered at no cost to the employee, vest over five years and pay a significant return if Pepsi's stock increases during that period. The potential return, given the firm's history of stock appreciation, is hundreds of thousands of dollars for a midlevel employee. One of the architects of the program commented, "A lot of companies are saying they want to give employees a sense of ownership. But providing a sense of ownership is like providing a sense of lunch: you can smell it, you can look at it, and you can help decide what to eat but you can't eat it. At PepsiCo, the company shows a real commitment to the concept of sharing ownership broadly."[15] Pepsi's leadership believes that because the company is selling small items—a drink, a bag of snacks, a pizza—employees are essential in ensuring high-quality interaction with its millions of customers. Its program and the concern it makes tangible help ensure that quality.

Demonstrating Concern at Hewlett-Packard

Every firm ultimately develops its own unique approach to demonstrating concern while delivering bottom-line results. Consider the actions of HP with respect to support, stability, and familiarity as an illustration of what one exemplary firm does to build trust through concern.

The founders of HP wanted to build a company whose leaders took direct responsibility for their relationship with employees. As a result, HP did not have a human resources department for the first twenty years of its existence. In the late 1950s, they decided the time had come to have a corporate personnel department with a narrowly defined charter of supporting the management team (who, in turn, would support the employees). The founders were clear that HR was in no way to supplant the manager-employee relationship that they considered so vital to the firm's success. While HP has strayed at times from this narrow definition, the firm has tried to ensure that HR does not become a "third party" that gets in the way of familiarity between leaders and employees. This effort has made a difference in keeping leadership at all levels in close touch with employees at all levels of the organization.

Supporting Employees

In addition to this base of connection and support, HP offers flexible work practices to accommodate personal demands on employees' time.

Flexible Work Practices

HP tries to accommodate its employees whenever possible in terms of work preferences. For example, people's preferences about location are solicited and honored when they can be. People are also given options around telecommuting (if possible given the job), job sharing, and part-time work. The firm has implemented a flex-time approach that allows employees to come to work during a window of three hours in the morning and work a set number of hours (resulting in a full eight-hour day). HP recognizes the individuality of its employees and that a "one size fits all" approach to managing people will not work in today's world. It sees flexibility as key to meeting employee needs and, to the degree possible, tries to understand and adapt to those needs.

As Packard writes, "to my mind, flextime is the essence of respect for and trust in people. It says that we both appreciate that our people have busy personal lives and that we trust them to devise, with their supervisor or work group, a schedule that is personally convenient yet fair to others."[16]

Personal Time

HP was one of the first firms to combine vacation time with sick leave. Today, HP's employees receive a pool of time that combines vacation time with sick leave; each employee then decides how to use the days. HP implemented this approach because in the past, people had needed to justify sick time in order to use it. This created problems because some employees needed time off when they were neither sick nor on vacation (for example, to care for a child or parent). So some employees would call in sick when they were not simply because of the way the system was set up. In a none-too-subtle way, the system encouraged lying. In addition, those who abused the system by feigning illness in order to take a longer vacation, for example, received benefits that were not offered to those who followed the rules. The old approach had distrust built into it. Supervisors had to spend time considering whether someone was actually sick or not. Employees, in some cases, felt they could not tell the truth regarding their need for personal time.

To remedy the situation, HP took the average sick time across the company and created the new "pooled time" plan. The cost to the company was zero because HP based the new plan on historical use of sick leave. Moreover, HP eliminated a situation that created distrust within a firm that places high value on trust.

Offering Employment Stability

HP does not have a policy against layoffs but does try to provide employment security whenever possible. There have been reductions in the workforce over the past decade, but HP has gone to great lengths to avoid them. Instead, the firm will, if necessary, reduce hiring in new areas and move people as appropriate to fill new positions. If a division is going through a downsizing, the corporation provides a great deal of support in helping people to find new positions and in helping to relocate them. While the policy of giving existing employees preference in hiring decisions can cause some tension, its long-term benefits are significant.

Hewlett-Packard's founders wanted people who shared their goals of making a profit and a contribution. In turn, they intended to provide employees with opportunity and job security as best they could. Early on, they made the important decision not to be "a 'hire and fire'—a company that would seek large, short-term contracts, employ a great many people for the duration of the contract, and at its completion let those people go." They didn't want to operate that way. Instead, they "wanted to be in the business for the long haul, to have a company built around a stable and dedicated workforce."[17] And their goals have been met, in part through their concern.

Ensuring Deep Familiarity

Through techniques for business dialogue, space sharing, and management, as well as through planned social events, Hewlett-Packard sustains familiarity and demonstrates concern quite clearly.

Business Dialogue

Much of HP's communication focuses on the performance of the business and its impact on customers and employees. In particular, twice a year, senior leadership reviews the firm's overall results and distributes a profit-sharing payout. Senior leadership meets regularly with employees in informal lunches. The firm also sends out electronic news bulletins to keep people informed of key events. In addition, HP employees use intranet and electronic news groups to share information and exchange points of view.

Shared Physical Space

As noted earlier, HP designs its offices and plants with an open layout and discourages the use of executive offices of any kind. Managers are encouraged to work in the same area with their employees. Offices are designed to be open, and people are encouraged to interact as much as possible with their colleagues.

Constant Contact

HP's "management by walking around" (MBWA) and open-door policies underscore the familiarity in the firm's culture. HP's well-known "management by walking around" is a simple yet effective way to ensure that the firm's leaders and employees stay in constant contact. The informality of such an approach allows "nonagenda" items to surface and be discussed. It also increases the perception that leadership is involved in the business and understands the real issues that have an impact on customers and employees.

HP's open-door policy allows people to go one level above their current supervisor to voice a concern or issue (and to do so with confidentiality assured). More important, the culture is one of approachability: most people feel they can call anyone in the firm if they have a concern.

Social Events

Any review of HP's history turns up photographs of company picnics with the founders serving food to the assembled. From the beginning, HP has encouraged a family-like atmosphere in which people get together informally as individuals, teams, or in larger groups. The result is greater familiarity and comfort with people working at different levels and in different groups.

Those looking to HP for answers to the dilemmas of trust will find a rich example of what one firm has done to demonstrate concern while delivering impressive financial results. Those at HP have met the underlying challenge in demonstrating concern: their decisions are employee friendly while ultimately enhancing shareholder value and building competitive advantage. By consciously communicating across all levels, Hewlett-Packard ensures familiarity throughout the organization. Through their demonstrated concern for employees, they are able to attract and retain talented people; they are also able to foster collaboration within the organization.

But as in other areas of organizational life, simple mimicry will fail to produce similar results. It is often the interplay among various organizational practices and norms that produces the net result. Thus, taking one aspect of the HP Way and introducing it into one's own organization will most likely fail. Each organization must develop culture-appropriate mechanisms with a deep basis of support; these must be more than superficial techniques. Even though the technique alone may work, it must fit the particular culture of an organization if it is to survive over time.

∽

Providing Support

Demonstrating concern was far easier in the 1980s when competitive pressures were less intense. Today's unrelenting focus on short-term profits, along with a much more competitive global economy, has resulted in organizational changes that have violated the expectations of many employees with regard to mutual concern and loyalty. Downsizing is the most visible of these changes. The challenge is to demonstrate concern while implementing the necessary changes that often erode trust.

Leaders seeking to build high-trust cultures must create organizational structures and processes that foster ownership at the local level, providing organizational members with a high degree of control over their own fate. The goal is to move away from a centralized approach where a few people control the organization's resources and replace it with a distributed ownership in which everyone feels and acts like an owner. Critical to this goal are the following elements of concern:

- One vision, one company
- Confidence in people's ability
- Familiarity and dialogue
- Recognition of contributions

Unstated in these elements but at their foundation is the importance of leadership and structure.

It is a painful lesson but one that must be learned: retaining absolute power in the hands of a few can never produce the level of concern that is needed to sustain trust. Even under the best of circumstances, the result will be a paternalistic approach that will ultimately frustrate all involved. In other words, the answer is not to wield power in a "kinder and gentler manner" but—to the degree appropriate—to give people control of their own fate in helping to create a profitable business.

Demonstrating Concern Survey

Assessing Your Organization or Team

To assess the degree to which your organization or team meets the imperative of demonstrating concern, complete the following survey. The contrasting statements are designed to provoke your thinking regarding the level of performance in your organization and its impact on trust. For each statement, indicate which point along the continuum most accurately describes your organization or team.

You can use your ratings to spot areas in need of improvement. The total at the bottom of the page provides a general indication of concern in your organization or team, while the ratings on individual questions provide more detailed feedback. You can also transfer your overall rating in this chapter to Resource One to develop an overall trust profile of your organization or team.

Demonstrating Concern

Assessing Your Organization or Team

In this organization (or team) . . .

People feel like they are caught among groups in constant conflict		People feel like they are part of "one firm" and share a common vision
The way people are treated would make you think they are incompetent		There is faith in the ability of people at all levels to accomplish great things
People are restricted by a variety of controls and policies		People have the autonomy and power needed to meet their business objectives
People are rarely recognized for the contributions they make		People are regularly recognized for the contributions they make
Only the senior people benefit financially if we meet our business targets		Everyone benefits financially if we meet our business targets
People have "hidden agendas" and don't deal honestly with each other		People are open with information and honest about their motives
People have almost no contact with senior leadership		Leadership is accessible and open to input from all levels
Overall, our leaders care primarily about themselves		Overall, our leaders care about and support people at every level

Total Score: ____

Low concern: 8–18; Moderate concern: 19–29; High concern: 30–40

Part Three

Creating Trust-Based Organizations

Part Three introduces the key leverage points for building organizations that sustain trust over the long term. These are the larger issues that must be addressed in order to meet the imperatives of results, integrity, and concern. This section outlines the leadership behavior and organizational mechanisms needed to build trust.

In the three chapters of this section, I highlight several key themes:

1. The actions of leaders at all levels significantly influence trust. Senior leaders are particularly powerful in creating or eroding trust. Those seeking to build high-trust cultures must develop a group of leaders whose actions reflect the importance of each of the trust imperatives—and who are capable of balancing these imperatives when they conflict.

2. An organization's formal structures and processes can build trust or destroy it, just as leaders can. Those seeking to create trust-based organizations must look at a firm's structures, management processes, policies, and practices. Each can be assessed in terms of its impact on trust within the organization (that is, is it trust sustaining, trust neutral, or trust eroding?). In most cases, firms have formal arrangements, such as restrictive guidelines, that limit employee autonomy and reveal the distrust that leadership has for employees.

3. The culture of an organization reflects the informal aspects of how a firm operates. Some firms, for example, are averse

to conflict and discourage honest communication in a variety of ways. As with structure, elements of a firm's culture can support or erode trust over time. The goal is to create a culture that reinforces the trust imperatives outlined in Part Two.

In sum, Chapters Six, Seven, and Eight provide a set of principles for designing and building organizations that are capable of sustaining trust over time.

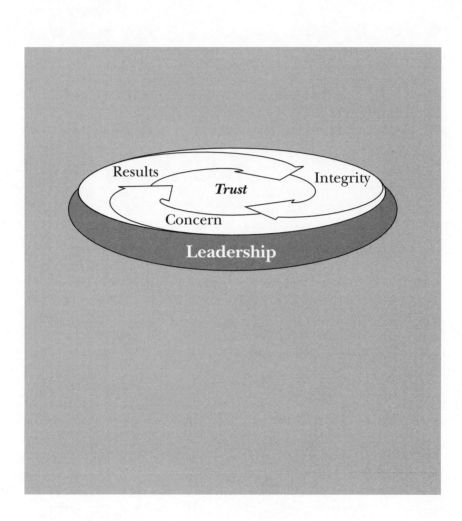

Chapter Six

Building Trust Through Leadership

The three imperatives of achieving results, acting with integrity, and demonstrating concern simplify a complex set of factors that contribute to trust and distrust. Of course, building an organization or team capable of realizing these imperatives is difficult even under the best of circumstances. Achieving results in today's increasingly competitive business environment demands more skill and discipline than at any time in the past. And mastering the tradeoffs among results, integrity, and concern places enormous demands on even the most successful organizations and their leaders.

In many ways, organizational trust begins and ends with the actions of leadership. Indeed, trust is based on the caliber of leadership within a firm or team. To better understand trust, we can start by examining the personal attributes and behavior of an organization's current and past leaders. Highly credible leaders can, through the shear impact of their individual influence, overcome distrust and create a trust-based environment. In contrast, incompetent or unethical leaders can quickly erode whatever trust exists within an organization or team.

Beyond personally behaving in a trustworthy way, senior leadership must build credible groups at various points in an organization's structure. Increasingly, those reporting directly to the chief executive officer or president need to act in a highly effective and coordinated way if trust is to be sustained throughout the organization. The senior leader is uniquely responsible for building an effective senior leadership group that can fulfill the trust imperatives of results, integrity, and concern. More generally, the senior leader must also support the development of effective groups at other levels, each with oversight and performance responsibilities. The type and number of these groups will vary from one firm to next. Typically they include the board of directors, business unit and functional leadership teams, and key project and task teams.

The leader must be the primary designer of organizational processes, both formal and informal, that will work to overcome distrust and sustain appropriate levels of trust. In other words, effective senior leaders assume the role of organizational architects. This role involves the creation of a viable competitive strategy, the development of a core set of guiding principles and values, the macro design of organizational structures, the delineation of the accountabilities of key individuals and leadership groups, and the selection of a leadership cadre to fill those roles. The senior leader must also ensure that appropriate controls are in place to prevent abuses by individuals or groups that could harm the larger organization and its members. The primary tasks to be undertaken by trustworthy leadership are outlined in Exhibit 6.1; these tasks are discussed in this chapter and those that follow.

Exhibit 6.1. Leadership and Trust: The Primary Tasks.

Personally Model Trustworthy Leadership
- Achieve results
- Act with integrity
- Demonstrate concern

Build Trustworthy Leadership Groups
- Board of directors
- Senior leadership team
- "Top 100" leaders
- Key groups

Develop Trust-Sustaining Organizational Mechanisms
- Organizational architecture
- Organizational culture

Establishing Credibility at the Top

Organizational trust clearly begins with the credibility of the senior leader. As Thomas Kaney, vice president of Smith-Kline Becham, remarked, "to achieve deep-level change in large corporations, you need leadership at all levels that is both trusting and trustworthy. The key to our success since our merger several years ago has been our senior leadership's ability to set a clear direction and then trust our people to deliver. In turn, leadership must act in a manner that sustains trust in them as leaders. People will only follow those whom they believe are credible and worthy of their trust." Trust, then, is key in getting people to follow the direction articulated by leadership. It is, as Bennis and Nanus state, "the emotional glue that binds followers and leaders together. The accumulation of trust is a measure of legitimacy of leadership. It cannot be mandated or purchased; it must be earned. Trust is the basic ingredient of all organizations, the lubrication that maintains the organization."[1]

The critical role of leadership is clear when examining a founder's impact, positive or negative, on the level of trust within a firm. In some cases, the founder's legacy with regard to trust can last for decades. As a positive example, we've seen that Bill Hewlett's and David Packard's actions created a set of practices and values that have fostered a high trust level within HP over the past fifty years. As a negative example, one large corporation with which I have worked had especially high levels of distrust in many of its divisions. A number of factors contributed to this, but a primary influence appeared to be the distrustful leadership style of the firm's founder—who had died many decades earlier. Those who were aware of the firm's history observed that the founder had acted in unethical ways toward outside parties (such as customers, suppliers, competitors, and governmental agencies) as well as toward his own employees (such as members of his team, midlevel managers, and union members). His leadership style set a tone that far outlasted his personal involvement in the organization.

Since trust is built primarily on actions rather than pronouncements, nothing can undermine trust within an organization faster than a senior leader who is incompetent, unethical, or uncaring. Leaders need to act in ways that clearly demonstrate their commitment in each of the areas on which trust—and ultimately organizational performance—rests. The importance of modeling the trust imperatives (discussed in Chapters Three, Four, and Five) cannot be overstated. Leaders must achieve results, act with integrity, and demonstrate concern—all the while balancing these needs appropriately.

Leadership: Achieving Results

The first requirement of leadership is to ensure that the organization is competitively viable. In a business setting, trust begins by demonstrating the competence required for an organization or team to prosper and grow. This does not simply equate to technical skill, raw intelligence, or industry knowledge. It involves a constellation of attributes that fit the needs of a particular firm at a particular point in its history. For example, many rapidly growing organizations are led by entrepreneurs with enormous drive to achieve challenging performance milestones. Yet when the challenges shift to those of managing the organization's ever increasing size, this style of leadership can become less effective. The results will vary depending on the challenges facing an organization.

As an example of trust in leadership changing with the circumstances, consider the executive who leads his or her firm through a difficult period of restructuring and downsizing. This individual may be the savior of the firm, given the tough decisions that had been avoided for years by previous leaders. Yet this leader may not be the best one for the next phase of the firm's life, when growth in new and diverse markets is the key challenge. The leader who saved the firm from bankruptcy may be a poor fit with the challenges facing the restructured organization. Leaders, therefore, must provide the specific skills needed at a particular point in a firm's history.

Changeable as the basis of trust is, delivering the results expected is at the core of establishing trust in an organizational setting. It is not—and cannot be—detached from the everyday running of the business. Those who fail to deliver on their commitments will not be trusted as leaders or colleagues within most organizations and teams. Senior leaders must take responsibility for delivering on the key objectives that only they can perform. For example, most senior leaders must take responsibility for the long-range vision or strategy of the organization. Similarly, they must staff the senior levels of the organization and build an effective leadership team at the top. They must also uphold performance standards for those who report directly to them and for the organization as a whole.

Leaders must also set performance standards for themselves as leaders; ideally, these standards should be set high and should be specific rather than ambiguous. The pressures of increased competition, along with more activist boards and shareholders, have made leaders more deeply accountable for performance and concrete results than ever. Even without these pressures, a leader's credibility is enhanced by visibly holding to performance standards that are at least as stringent as those established for others.

Apple's recent turmoil suggests the importance of achieving results in sustaining trust in leadership. Michael Spindler's first two years as CEO of Apple were marked by a series of strategic and operational mistakes that crippled the firm and led to the widespread departure of senior talent. The firm failed, for example, to develop a viable strategic approach to licensing its operating system, which would have increased its share of the market. On an operational level, Apple badly miscalculated demand and found itself with either shortages or excess inventory. Spindler took control of a company in trouble—and soon found himself in charge of a situation that was going from bad to worse. He was unable to move Apple forward in an industry that was rapidly expanding on a global scale. As a result, he lost the confidence of individuals within the organization and key external shareholders who were dismayed at Apple's performance. Spindler could not recover the trust of those he was leading. His inability to deliver results eroded his credibility; he was forced to resign despite his desire for more time to implement his turnaround strategy. As his replacement, the board chose Gil Amelio, who has a reputation for achieving dramatic results in similarly difficult situations.

Leadership: Acting with Integrity

In addition to achieving results, leadership must act with integrity in order to be trusted. At its core, this involves complete honesty in relation to others within the organization. Indeed, in the 1980s and 1990s, at the top of the list in terms of what followers most often looked for in a leader was leadership honesty. In fact, this was

found to be the single most important ingredient in the leader-fol-
lower relationship.[2]

People often scrutinize the behavior of their leaders to assess
their level of honesty. Those who consistently act on what they say
fare well in this assessment. Integrity does not require absolute consistency across time and circumstances, but it does require alignment among values, words, and behavior. Those who change their
position depending on the audience they are addressing or the situation in which they find themselves, or who say one thing and do
another, are deemed in almost every situation to be untrustworthy.
For example, John Teets, the CEO of Dial, has recently come
under fire for what appear to be inconsistencies in what he believes
is good for his firm and how he behaves. In particular, Teets has a
well-earned reputation for cutting costs, keeping tight control of
company assets, and driving hard bargains with unions and suppliers. Yet his pay is far higher than that of CEOs in firms of similar size and market value. He has also spent money on corporate
jets, a new headquarters building, and local investments from
which he stands to benefit. Teets is being criticized for his apparent double standard with respect to Dial's money. This perception
of inconsistency, even if unfairly drawn, could erode Teets's credibility within the organization and with key external stakeholders.[3]

The dilemma of consistency is not isolated to a few senior leaders whose behavior is called into question. In today's fast-paced
world, all of us are under pressure to change our positions in order
to adapt to new information and new pressures. In doing so, we
risk appearing to be inconsistent and thus unworthy of trust. Consider the following examples:

•   A product development team commits to delivering a new
software program by the end of the calendar year. New competitive developments, however, require that additional features be
added to the program (otherwise, the product will arrive dead in
the water). The team moves forward, adding new features, under
the assumption that their actions are in the best interests of the
firm. Senior management reacts negatively to the delays and
blames the team for failing to deliver the product as promised.
Leadership perceives this failure as an inconsistency between what
the team said it would do and what it actually did, so it begins to
question the team's integrity and distrust its commitments, request-
ing detailed reviews of every checkpoint in the project.

- A firm with a history of paternalistic practices informs employees that their "no-layoff" policy will stay in effect, touting the need for loyalty in tough times. However, a severe decline in profitability forces leadership to violate this policy—and to do so quickly without getting much input from employees. While the layoffs are limited to 5 percent of the workforce, most feel that management lied and therefore cannot be trusted.

- A major manufacturing firm has spent years developing close working relationships with its customers. Foreign competitors, however, have captured market share through offering a high-value product (that is, a high-quality product offered at a low price). The U.S. firm responds by demanding that its suppliers cut their costs by 15 percent immediately or have their contracts terminated. A large majority of the suppliers agree under threat of losing business. But they are bitter that their customer, playing "hard ball" in order to cut costs, has violated a contract that had been negotiated only a few years before.

Each of these scenarios illustrates the potential downside of appearing to favor results over integrity (when integrity is broadly defined as coherence or consistency in one's actions). While dilemmas by their nature cannot be completely resolved, the situations just described could be managed in ways that would decrease the likelihood of distrust. Each involves collaborating with those who may see our actions as lacking integrity.

In the first case, the product development team failed to meet a launch schedule in order to improve the quality of their product. At the least, they could have informed others of the potential for delay and made sure that leadership understood the team's progress. They also could have brought senior management into the process of making decisions about the necessary time-versus-quality tradeoffs.

In the second case, senior managers made a mistake in committing to a policy that they might need to violate if market conditions changed. They also failed to bring others into the decision to violate the no-layoff policy. Instead, they could have created a team of employees and senior management to consider alternatives to address the crisis facing the organization. Collectively, the task force, representing the entire organization, could have made a decision that would achieve the same savings but without the negative consequences (for example, by using temporary layoffs or by helping to place employees with other nearby firms). Clearly, this solution would not be possible in all situations, since rapid decisive action is sometimes essential.

In the third case, the manufacturing firm could have articulated a clear savings goal and then worked with their suppliers to reach that objective. Those who could not reach the targets would be dropped as suppliers over time—but not before the firm had worked with them in a collaborative manner to try to reach the stated goal.

Beyond modeling integrity, leaders are also responsible for holding others to the same standard, for requiring that *everyone* in the organization act with integrity. Leaders must take the initiative and remove those who do not uphold a firm's values; no one else can do so. As Pete Peterson of Hewlett-Packard said, "we will move very quickly on people who violate our principles. In particular, those who act in a manner that lacks integrity are removed immediately." This sounds extreme, but integrity is central to the HP Way, so action is critical. Employees are removed for any unethical business practice (such as misrepresenting financial results or product performance). Anything less would undermine the company's culture and the trust it sustains.

Leadership: Demonstrating Concern

People within the organization need to feel that they are more than a means to an end. Without demonstrated concern on the part of leadership, people may believe that leadership cares only about profit and will do whatever is required to make its quarterly targets. Establishing a shared vision is not an analytic exercise; rather, it shows people that leadership understands and cares about their well-being beyond their economic contribution. This is not to suggest a return to old forms of paternalism; instead, leaders must be aware of their influence in motivating people to strive toward a common objective. Leaders can reinforce the need for collective ownership of both the problems and their resolutions (versus the belief that senior management is solely responsible for an organization's problems and their resolutions).

Corporate leaders must resist any tendency to become isolated from their organizations. They need contact in order to understand what is happening in the organization, and they need the influence that comes with being available to others. Since a large part of leadership effectiveness requires that people believe their leaders are open to them as individuals and open to their point of view on the business, leaders do well to recognize that most people:

- Want the straight facts about their firm and its competitive standing
- Want to contribute to the organization's success and will strive to do a good job if they are properly supported
- Want to "own" a piece of the business and must be given the autonomy necessary to meet customer needs and address competitive trends
- Are more committed when they are treated as partners and owners with an important voice in how an organization is run (rather than human resources to be deployed as others see fit)
- Want to know their future prospects within an organization and how they are considered to be performing

Leaders need to recognize and integrate the views and concerns of others into how they run their business, demonstrating that these concerns have an influence on their actions.

Tom Wajnert, chair and CEO of AT&T Capital (now privately owned, this firm was formerly a business unit of AT&T), discussed the need for leadership to trust people in the organization:

> Our approach to trusting our members reflects, in part, my own personal beliefs about people. In particular, I believe people want to do a good job, and if properly supported, will do so. That approach is very different than the "command and control" philosophy you find in many firms. As a leader and a person, I have learned that we have far less control than we like to believe. I have had several events in my personal life, including the death of a spouse, that taught me the limits of our ability to control what occurs in our lives. These personal experiences have given me a different philosophy about leadership, which is much more about creating a shared sense of direction and responsibility. I'm convinced that my approach is more realistic in terms of how the world operates and ultimately more effective. I also sleep better at night knowing that I don't need to make all the decisions and that we have a management model that emphasizes shared accountability.

Trust requires that leaders act competently in helping their organizations to meet customer and shareholder expectations. Particularly in a demanding business environment, those acting competently may be perceived as lacking concern for those affected by their actions. Consider the following examples:

• A Fortune 100 firm decides that its competitive advantage lies in having superior leaders in every key position. Toward this end, the firm develops a world-class executive selection and development system. One feature of the program is an annual review of talent in the organization, with the intent, in part, of identifying those who are failing to meet performance expectations. Those who are failing are given feedback and coaching; if they continue to struggle, they are then moved out of the organization. Some people who are well liked but failing to meet expectations are fired. The system is seen as being punishing, and the organization is viewed as a "shark pit," where the only rule is survival of the fittest.

• An organization in a slow-changing industry now faces new Japanese competition that is dramatically rewriting the rules. They are bringing new products to market in half the time of those with dominant share. Senior management decides to act quickly to keep the Japanese from taking market share. They launch an initiative to reengineer the firm's core business processes; this results in some layoffs and widespread changes in people's responsibilities and reporting relationships. Most feel unsure about their new responsibilities and believe management acted too aggressively in making the changes. Most wonder what other changes are forthcoming and begin to distrust their firm's leadership.

• A functional leader has a technology development team reporting to her. This team must meet tight deadlines if the firm is to move forward with a new competitive offering. The team, unfortunately, has underperformed but feels that the problems reside elsewhere in the organization. The leader disagrees, as do her colleagues on the executive committee, and holds the team accountable for the project's shortcomings. As a result, team members receive no bonus and blame the functional leader. They begin to believe that she does not care about them or their point of view.

Each of these examples reflects a conflict among trust imperatives. The demands of balancing the need for results, integrity, and concern become the ultimate test that all leaders must face.

The tradeoffs among these imperatives are the focus of Chapter Nine. Steps that can be taken to manage the conflicts that emerge among these factors are discussed here.

Building Trustworthy Leadership Groups

Trust requires much more than just a senior person acting in a credible way. Trust begins with the senior leader, but it quickly becomes linked to the behavior of key leadership teams as well. Building trust therefore requires the development of highly effective leadership groups.

Most large organizations now have some type of leadership team at the top. While the effectiveness of these teams varies greatly, many are rife with distrust and unproductive political conflicts. These tensions can prevent leadership groups from agreeing on a common vision, dealing with tough business issues in a timely manner, and implementing strategy in a coordinated way. Today, the entire leadership team—including boards of directors, the most senior leaders, business unit or functional leadership teams, and specialized teams assigned to address key business challenges—must behave in a way that builds trust and overcomes distrust where it exists.

To create the most impact on trust, senior leaders must invest their time in building highly credible leader groups. The most immediate of these groups is the team of individuals reporting directly to the senior leader. The degree of teamwork should depend on the demands the organization faces. In some cases, the business, to be successful, requires close teamwork. In other cases, the team may be a loose collection of talented individuals who come together periodically to share information and coordinate the organization's general direction. Regardless of the composition or charge of this senior leadership team, its behavior is critical in building or eroding trust.

To sustain trust, the senior leadership team needs a common vision and business strategy. While there will inevitably be differences among team members, widely divergent views will result in a destructive malaise. Take, for example, the recent conflicts between the two top executives of Cable and Wireless, the British company offering telecommunications services. Lord Young (the chair) and James Ross (the chief executive and deputy chair) had feuded for almost a year over which of them should lead the company and in what direction. Ross was pushing to divest some of the company's investments in fifty-two countries—an empire that Young had built over the previous five years. In addition, by most accounts, the two men simply didn't like each other. As they quarreled over strategy and leadership roles, the company's stock price sagged in 1995, and Cable and Wireless came under increasing criticism for failing to institute a credible growth strategy in a highly competitive market. The conflict ended abruptly when the board took action to help unify the company and asked both men to step down.[4] There is speculation today that Cable and Wireless, given its vulnerable position in the highly competitive telecommunications industry, is actively looking to be acquired.

The situation at Cable and Wireless, while extreme, illustrates what occurs in many organizations. In the late 1970s and 1980s, Chrysler was an organization plagued with problems. In particular, Lee Iacocca came into a firm with thirty-five vice presidents, each with his or her own agenda and turf. He writes:

> Chrysler didn't really function like a company at all. Chrysler in 1978 was like Italy in the 1860s—the company consisted of a cluster of little duchies, each one run by a prima donna. It was a bunch of mini-empires, with nobody giving a damn about what anyone else was doing.[5]

Iacocca ended up removing thirty-three of the thirty-five VPs over a three-year period and in the process created management structures that gave the firm a more coordinated approach.

Alignment around strategic imperatives typically requires a shared view of competitive challenges and the direction of the industry in which one competes. The senior leader and senior team members must agree on a number of critical issues regarding the problems facing the organization and the path ahead. They should also agree on their role as a team in leading the organization. As a first step, they must consider and respond to a number of questions, briefly outlined here.

With respect to the team's charter and role:

- What is the purpose of the team?
- Who are its customers?
- What is the vital work that it must take on?

Given the team's charter,

- What competencies and skills are needed on the team?
- What is the appropriate number of team members?
- What are the informal agreements that guide how team members interact with each other?

In establishing operating principles and work processes,

- How will the team structure its work?
- How will it conduct meetings?
- How will it perform outside of meetings?

With respect to team goals, roles, and performance targets,

- What are the team's group-level goals and objectives?
- What unique roles do individuals play on the team?
- What is the unique role of the team leader?
- How will the performance of the leadership team be measured?
- How will the team enhance its own effectiveness?
- How will it stay in touch with the organization and with customers?

Once the group has been established and is operating, the standards used to assess its credibility should be similar to those used to assess leaders:

- Does the team exemplify the organization's highest values?
- Does the team have a great deal of credibility within the organization?
- Are the team and its members trusted by people and groups at all levels of the organization?

For a more detailed assessment, see Resource Two. Many of the questions posed there with respect to leadership credibility can easily be adapted to assess teams.

Developing Trust-Sustaining Mechanisms

Building trust is a paradoxical process. Trust results from doing many fundamental things right rather than from direct attempts to raise the level of trust within an organization or team. Thus, the most effective approaches to building trust are often those that focus on the actions that produce trust rather than on trust itself.

The evolution of Hewlett-Packard as a high-trust culture helps illustrate how a firm establishes and then sustains trust over a period of decades. Trust appears in one of the firm's value statements and is evident in some of the founders' writings—yet it is not a primary focus. Instead, the factors that lead to trust—factors such as winning in the marketplace, making a contribution, following through on commitments, and showing respect and concern for the well-being of others—are discussed under the banner of the "HP Way." Trust permeates much of the Hewlett-Packard culture but is not an end in itself.

Those seeking to build trust may thus be better served by going at it indirectly. The path to building trust is similar to that for building strong teams. Most successful team interventions focus on improving business performance—rather than simply on building the team or requiring teamwork. The team becomes the means by which a business objective is achieved; the team is not an end in itself. Those seeking to improve teamwork identify hard business challenges and provide new ways of helping the team function effectively in meeting those challenges. The fact that strong teams often exhibit high levels of trust is no coincidence. Both develop together, and they develop best when the focus is on performance and concrete results.

Whether a leader is trying to build a team or a high-performance organization, the goal is not simply to increase trust. The goal is to increase the likelihood of success by cultivating the appropriate level of trust in a given situation. Trust is a means of enhancing business performance over time. Blind trust or trust for the sake of trust should not be the goal.

Trust is often won or lost during periods of adversity that test the foundation on which trust is built. For example, in the early 1970s, Hewlett-Packard created a reservoir of trust in its workforce by implementing a temporary reduction in work hours across the board, rather than suffer through a round of permanent layoffs. Faced with a recession and a resulting excess of employees, Hewlett-Packard's approach, which became a highly visible model of innovative reaction to market pressures, required that employees take every other Friday off without pay. The altered schedule lasted for six months, until the demand in the marketplace was sufficient to warrant full utilization of the production staff. This approach became a powerful symbol of Hewlett-Packard's ability to balance concern for the bottom line with concern for the well-being of its workforce.

While it is certainly true that trust can be won or lost during difficult times, few organizations or teams can sustain high levels of trust in the face of ongoing adversity or failure. In general, when one is building a high-trust culture, adversity is better in small doses. Chronic organizational decline or failure inevitably results in higher levels of suspicion and in actions that ultimately erode trust. Efforts to build trust in these environments are often overwhelmed by the larger dynamics of organizational decline. The impact of failure is felt in terms of declining morale, reduced financial rewards, reorganizations, and downsizing. Thus, the first responsibility of those seeking to build trust is to make every effort to ensure the success of the team or organization. This does not mean that results should be gained or jump-started in a way that lacks integrity or that erodes the goodwill of team members or others in the organization. It does mean that trust ultimately rests on a foundation of business results and growth. The bottom line: there are few failing organizations with high levels of trust.

Leading the Way to Trust

Then how do leaders encourage trust? How do leaders help the team or organization increase its depth and scope of trust? Tom Wajnert of AT&T Capital speaks to this question and underscores the importance of trust in relation to strong business fundamentals:

> Trusting your people is important within the context of a viable business model. In some cases, the senior leader needs to take control and fix the fundamentals before you begin working on trust. This may require approaches that don't build trust in the short run. But trust, without a sound business strategy, is absurd.

Those seeking to improve trust should first focus on the business outcomes that their organization or team must achieve and on a few core initiatives that if successfully implemented, will result in success.

In striving to create high-trust organizations, leaders must keep in mind that trust is but one *means* of achieving the ultimate goal of organizational and team results; it is not the desired end. Nor should it become the focus. Since trust always exists in relation to distrust, to raise the issue of trust can raise the possibility, or even desirability, of distrust; a focus on trust can therefore inadvertently raise the level of distrust within an organization or team. This is not to suggest that trust should become a taboo subject. But leaders should take care; people become suspicious if they believe their trust is being forced or manipulated.

Instead, trust appears to function most effectively in the background. As a start, effective leaders should personally model appropriate behavior in relation to the three trust imperatives of results, integrity, and concern. Yet difficult as it is to do, acting in a credible manner is insufficient in order to build and sustain trust. Those seeking to create high-trust organizations must take the next step of spreading trust through the organization via leadership groups. Balancing the often-competing demands of these trust imperatives is difficult enough; simultaneously balancing the demands of role modeling, building teams, and designing trust-sustaining systems and practices is an extraordinary challenge.

The 3M company, for example, has created a culture that fosters trust among individuals and groups in developing innovative new products. Its CEO, Desi DeSimone, underscores leadership's role in creating the high-trust culture a firm needs to sustain a high level of innovation. He believes that if senior management has "internalized the principles," it can then "create a trust relationship in the company." When "innovation and respect for the individual" are central to the culture, the "top knows it should trust the process of bottom-up innovation by leaving a crack open when someone is insistent that a blocked project has potential." In turn, the lower levels trust the top when these leaders intervene or control their activities.[6]

~~

Balancing Leadership Demands

Leadership's role in building high-trust organizations involves three related tasks:

- Personally modeling trustworthy behavior
- Building trustworthy leadership teams
- Developing trust-sustaining organizational practices

Balancing the demands presented by these tasks is no small challenge. Leaders must personally exhibit trustworthy and trusting behavior. At the same time, they must direct their attention to the architecture (the structures and procedures that formally influence how a group operates) and the culture (the informal values, rules, and operating principles) of organizational life. Both are equally important and must be integrated appropriately for an organization or team to function well. In short, trustworthy leadership is a perpetual and fast-paced balancing act. The next two chapters offer helpful approaches to building trust through organizational architecture and culture.

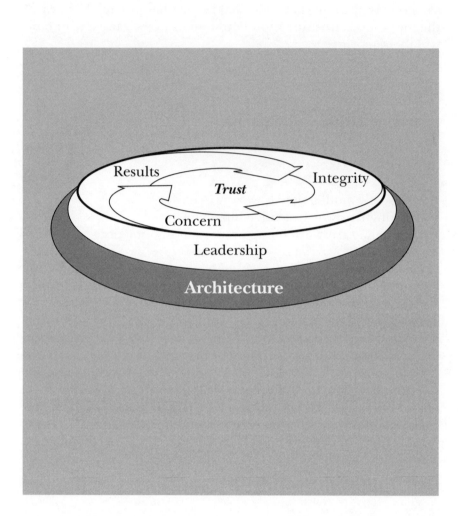

Chapter Seven

Building Trust Through Organizational Architecture

The behavior of leaders, individually and collectively, has a major impact on trust. As important, however, are the formal and informal aspects of organizational life that promote or erode trust over time. Building organizations that sustain trust requires an understanding of the firm-level dynamics that shape relationships among people. All told, building trust requires attention to the design and management of organizational structures and processes.

It's worth taking some time to consider the factors that erode trust. When one management consultant explored trust levels with a group of managers, he and they quickly learned a lot about the organizational side of trust. The consultant asked the managers to describe the actions and procedures that would create a low-trust organization. In no time, the managers had a list: "Make sure that everything is locked up. . . . Introduce voluminous manuals of operating procedures. . . . Fire people without warning. . . . Hold private meetings to which most people are not invited." It was a telling and familiar list. "One by one, the managers . . . flushed with embarrassment, recognized that they were describing aspects of their own organizations."[1] This is an important lesson—one to remember in designing the supporting architecture for your organization.

Every organization and team face a unique set of challenges that determines the details of how trust is built or destroyed. A firm's history is particularly important in shaping people's expectations and their general inclination to trust or distrust others. Similarly, the business environment in which each organization or team operates results in a specific set of pressures and dilemmas that have an impact on trust levels within the organization. Trust exists in relation to a particular set of constraints that are unique to each organization and team. Yet a set of general principles can help those seeking to foster the trust necessary to support high performance.

Note that in using these prescriptions, you should first evaluate the specific challenges facing your team or organization and then modify your actions in order to meet your group's particular needs. These recommendations and the principles behind them will be useful in organizations or teams in which the level of trust is at least moderate and in which distrust, where it does exist, has not reached a breaking point. Recommendations for crisis situations are discussed in Chapter Ten.

Developing the Architecture of Trust

Formal approaches to building trust involve an organization's objectives, structures, and management processes. There are a number of important actions to take:

• *Promote aggressive business targets.* People must agree on targets toward which they can work wholeheartedly.

• *Develop aligned performance accountabilities.* Accountabilities must be clear and uncomplicated—yet general enough to allow unfettered action.

• *Build high-ownership organizational structures.* Such structures should emphasize local authority.

• *Ensure superior talent at every level.* Seek out and actively reinforce talent through assessment and selection, developmental strategies, and performance decisions.

• *Maintain systems to share information.* People in each group and at every level must have the business information necessary to fulfill their responsibilities and work toward their goals.

• *Institute a few rigorous strategic controls.* Controls, often running in the background, are necessary to monitor performance and outcomes. When put in place properly, they can increase both the likelihood of predictable results and the levels of trust.

The following sections discuss each of these actions in turn. There are, as you will see, natural connections among them. The organization that recognizes these connections and links them together adds enormously to its strength and flexibility by increasing levels of trust.

Promoting Aggressive Business Targets

In order to extend their trust, most people need to believe that others are pursuing an agenda or set of objectives similar to their own. One way of increasing this alignment of interests and priorities is to agree on desired business outcomes first. Shared commitment to aggressive targets can also increase the likelihood of people pulling together in an effort to realize a common goal. This is one reason we see higher levels of trust during times of crisis: people unite around a single objective and, as a result, focus less on their individual differences. Those seeking to build trust in organizations and teams should develop higher-order goals around which people can rally. In some cases, the higher-order goal may be an ambitious business objective that requires the support of all organizational or team members. GE, for example, focuses on what their CEO describes as big dreams—not the decimal points of budget forecasts. As CEO Welch writes, "we don't tell people what to do or how to do it. [We] give them big targets, let them dream, reach for them and do it their way. We find that every day, by not telling people what to do, they do a hell of a lot better than they would've if we had told them what to do."[2] Welch argues that the task for leadership is to get people "in the game" by creating stretch objectives and ambitious dreams of what the future can hold.

Stretch objectives are increasingly common in most organizations and teams. Bristol-Myers Squibb, for example, has publicly launched an effort to double revenue and profit by the year 2000. This "double-double" objective, if managed skillfully, can bring people together and result in higher levels of cooperation and trust. Other examples include WalMart's goal of doubling sales by the year 2000, Motorola's ambition to reach Six Sigma quality standards, and Chrysler's desire to be the leading automotive company in the world.

Stretch objectives can, of course, result in suspicion and hostility if people feel that they are being forced to accept an impossible task or are being asked to achieve an ambitious goal without the proper support or tools. A process needs to be in place to ensure that the stretch objectives are owned by those who must meet them and by those to whom they report. This, of course, may require dramatic shifts in how an organization is structured and how it develops performance objectives. Forcing aggressive objectives on people or failing to provide them with the autonomy or resources they need to succeed will only result in failure and more distrust.

Developing Aligned Performance Accountabilities

Trust is valuable because it allows us to keep many options open on *how* we achieve a particular outcome. But agreement about the mutually desired outcome is essential. Indeed, trust requires clear, not overly complicated agreements about what each party will deliver in a given setting. These agreements are needed to avoid conflict later when events suggest that one or both parties in the relationship failed to meet the expectations of the others.

Many of the businesses with which I work as a consultant use decentralized business units. In the best cases, the leaders of the corporation and the heads of the business units have established a clear set of expectations regarding the results expected from each. The business unit leaders need and respond well to a clear set of measurable performance targets that they have helped craft and that they fully own. These leaders have learned that trust is not a soft issue, unrelated to the setting of clear accountabilities. They understand that expectations in each of the areas that promote trust—achieving results, acting with integrity, and demonstrating concern—are critical in determining whether trust is gained or lost. They understand that responsibilities and performance targets must be clearly delineated.

Those seeking high-trust relationships must be clear about the key outcomes expected and the measures that will be used to measure those outcomes. GE, for example, puts great effort into clarifying performance expectations for all of its divisions. There is particular emphasis on a few key measures, such as cash flow, customer satisfaction, and employee satisfaction. But the general goal in each of GE's divisions is to dominate its industry. These guidelines serve as the framework around which performance is measured; they work in place of more detailed and rigid control mechanisms.

Clarifying expectations is important because when people assume different outcomes, suspicion results. Exactly how to make expectations clear is part of the balancing act that leadership faces: too much detail and people are left with no independence or incentive; too little detail and chances of mistakes increase. A legalistic approach to stipulating all contingencies and the rights and duties of each party moves us away from a trust relationship and into the realm where each party assumes that the other will act in a trustworthy manner only if rigid constraints have been stipulated. In most situations, there is an inverse relationship between the use of rules and regulations and a healthy level of trust: the more people depend on rigid rules to regulate their relationships, the less they trust each other.[3] Instead, agreements should be general enough to allow each party considerable room in determining how to achieve the results desired.

Building High-Ownership Organizational Structures

A great deal of the distrust we see in large corporations arises because of the small degree of control given to those closest to the customers and competitors. If those held accountable for performance are limited in what they can do to achieve results, they will distrust those who are putting them into this "double bind."[4] They are told that they must deliver certain results but then are not given the resources or authority to do so (the first bind). Then they are told directly, or more often indirectly, that they cannot talk about the situation and its dynamics (the second bind). This sets up a pattern in which people are frustrated but cannot deal with it directly.

One way of developing clear accountabilities and the authority needed to deliver results is to create self-contained, relatively small units within larger corporate structures. The 3M company, throughout its history, has exhibited a bias toward small entrepreneurial organizations. This approach, which they call a "grow and divide" strategy, creates new units out of existing units as the latter introduce new products and services. The purpose of this technique is to ensure sufficient focus on new products and markets (which can get lost in larger, more mature businesses). The new organizations are given clear growth targets but are allowed a great deal of autonomy in running their operations.

Johnson & Johnson also has a rich history of autonomous business units. Beginning in the early part of this century, Johnson & Johnson developed a model that establishes each new product or service as an independent entity (once that product reaches a certain size and scope, as at 3M). Today, there are over 160 separately chartered companies within the corporation. Ralph Larson, CEO of Johnson & Johnson, notes, "We will never give up the principles of decentralization, which is to give our operating executives ownership of the business. They are ultimately responsible."[5]

The large engineering firm of ASEA Brown Boveria (ABB) is another company that believes that small profit centers are extremely effective as a means of organization. Within ABB, a typical profit center is made up of fifty people. In total, there are 1,300 companies and 50,000 profit centers. This structure allows for minimum corporate staff; there are only 250 corporate executives for a corporation of 200,000 people. The firm provides its profit centers with a great deal of autonomy, with the corporate leadership group working to sustain a core set of values and disseminate knowledge and best practices as needed.[6]

The creation of self-contained integrated units is also important within groups or divisions. Distrust often results from functional structures that are so narrow that they create conflict among those trying to accomplish their tasks. An example of the shift away from these types of structures is found in United Airlines, which recently reorganized its maintenance center in San Francisco into an integrated set of stand-alone businesses. The new federation is made up of self-sufficient product centers, each including mechanics, engineers, planners, and administrators. Each center has nearly total responsibility for performance in its own product area and is provided with the resources and autonomy needed to accomplish its goals.[7]

With clear accountabilities must come localized control over as many of the factors that influence performance as possible. The connection between accountabilities and trust is clear at Hewlett-Packard. There, the policy is to split off operations when they become too large, a policy that they call "local decentralization." The goal is to provide a large measure of autonomy to each division and to foster individual motivation, initiative, and creativity in order to provide "wide latitude of freedom in working toward common goals and objectives." In addition, as Packard has emphasized, decentralization helps "each division to retain and nurture the kind of intimacy, the caring for people, and the ease of communication that were characteristic of the company when it was smaller."[8]

Hewlett-Packard's individual businesses produce and sell thousands of products. There are more than 650 plants and offices in over 120 countries worldwide. Each is given a great deal of leeway in running its operations because, as HP's founders made clear, the company's success "depends in large part on giving the responsibility to the level where it can be exercised effectively, usually at the lowest possible level of the organization, the level nearest the customer." HP has established processes to ensure that employees have "flexibility in working toward common goals"; the employees can thus help determine what is best for their operation and their organization.[9]

The revitalization of one of Hewlett-Packard's test and measurement divisions points out the benefits of autonomy. The division's future looked bleak because spending in its core business—defense and aerospace—was rapidly declining. Because it was an autonomous division within Hewlett-Packard, it had the power to alter its vision. It proposed to move into the video and broadcast television market. Over a several-year period, the division completely rebuilt itself around a different set of products and customers. Some described the move as from "crew cuts to ponytails." It subsequently became one of the fastest-growing areas within Hewlett-Packard, approaching over 20 percent increases in annual sales and revenue. As the division manager at the time observed, "none of this could have happened outside the current environment of Hewlett-Packard."[10]

Ensuring Superior Talent

Trust is more likely when an organization or team is staffed by people with the requisite skills and ability. A high-trust organization requires superb talent at each level. Indeed, trust cannot be sustained in those organizations and teams with only mediocre talent. Talent involves technical and managerial ability as well as integrity and concern in how one approaches work. Steve Kerr, vice president of corporate management development at GE, summarized the importance of talent in a high-trust culture: "You can't run a boundaryless organization without superb people. Our systems are designed to identify and then develop those with the greatest potential—and we have some of the best people in world. Our people need to be world class to handle all that we give them."

Most organizations recognize the need for superb talent, but only a few actually develop the rigorous processes needed to create strong leaders. To have more than just a few good leaders, to develop superior talent across the organization, three factors are generally needed: assessment and selection, developmental strategies, and performance decisions.

Assessment and Selection

Pete Peterson of Hewlett-Packard believes that selection is more important in a high-trust culture than in firms with lower levels of trust. As he said,

> A high-trust culture means that you cannot take just anyone in the hiring process. Our organization works only if we hire highly qualified people with the right values and principles. That doesn't mean we are all alike; in fact, we have an extremely diverse workforce. However, we screen people through very tough interviews. For example, we make people demonstrate their skill level in our interviews. We also do drug testing. The intent behind these approaches is to ensure that we hire people who can function in our high-trust environment.

Organizations need a systematic process by which talent can be assessed and appropriate actions taken (whether that action be advancement to a more challenging position or removal from the firm). Motorola, like HP, puts new job candidates through days of interviews with people at various levels, rigorous tests of ability and knowledge, along with more general written compositions. At Southwest Airlines, selection of new hires is a time-consuming process that is not rushed in spite of the firm's rapid growth. Employees—whether pilots or mechanics—are hired based on studies that identify the key attributes for success, which include a willingness to work as part of a team. The result is a cohesive workforce with a turnover rate that is about half the industry average.[11]

Once people are on board, their performance and future potential must be evaluated with the same type of rigor. Firms such as Pepsi, GE, AlliedSignal, and Johnson & Johnson have developed disciplined approaches to evaluating their leadership talent over time.

Developmental Strategies

Even firms with rigorous selection and assessment processes may have little in the way of developmental strategies. These strategies should begin with the initial socialization of new members and continue through the senior leadership ranks. The best firms actively support development, even though it is also viewed as the responsibility of each individual. Encouragement and opportunity are provided for those ambitious enough to push their own development. For example, Fred Meyer, a West Coast discount chain with more than $3 billion in annual sales, has placed training PCs in all of its stores. CD-ROM minicourses, of twenty to forty minutes each, are required of all employees.[12] Or consider the firm's Learn and Earn Program, developed to encourage continuous learning. Employees are rewarded for reading business-related books or videos during their off hours. A list of books and tapes is distributed with an assigned value to each (for example, when an employee submits a one-page report on her reactions to reading *Reengineering the Corporation,* she will receive $30).[13]

Senior management will also become actively involved in the progress of the top two hundred to five hundred people in the organization, and those at lower leadership levels will do the same. At GE, for example, Welch plays an active role in the development process. As one executive noted, "Welch knows in some detail most of the top 1,100 in the organization and will become upset if he feels that we are not doing our part to develop them through stretch assignments." Development must be an ongoing daily task closely linked to the real-time challenges facing the business.

The likelihood of trust increases when organizations have developed both formal and informal approaches to learning from experience. A key is to deal with problems in a direct, honest, and even tough way—but without damaging or making scapegoats out of those involved in failed efforts. The senior leader, in particular, sets the tone in terms of how the organization deals with failure. There are, of course, leaders who do not want to hear bad news. There are also those who will listen to bad news and then proceed to punish those involved. In these firms, those involved in failing efforts fear for their careers, so they will attempt to hide failures or to distance themselves from them. Instead, the goal should be to treat failure with the seriousness it deserves but without creating a culture in which people will not examine failed efforts in order to learn from them.

Performance Decisions

Most important, the large majority of firms lack the conviction needed to make the difficult decisions about those who are not meeting performance expectations. Too many organizations and teams accept substandard or mediocre performance over a long period of time. Perhaps employees are not achieving the agreed-on results (and excuses for lack of success are easily found). Or perhaps a leader ignores the firm's values and operating principles while delivering financial results (and the apparent violation of the firm's principles is tolerated). These inconsistencies erode people's faith in each other. Whenever a significant number of people are unable or unwilling to fulfill their responsibilities, the organization as a whole will be low on trust.

It is a common mistake: people often overlook the importance of building superior talent in the creation of a high-trust culture. This presents two challenges. The first challenge is to take the tough actions that will build the necessary knowledge and skill. Despite the fact that big business has a reputation for being ruthless, I have found that most organizations and most leaders refuse to make the tough calls on people. Yet if people fail to deliver the results they promise, if they act without integrity or consistency, or if they show little or no concern for the well-being of others yet they suffer no negative consequences in terms of their career or rewards, then the trust of others in the organization deteriorates. Once trust is violated in this way, the cycle of distrust can permeate an entire team or organization. To remedy this situation, leaders must take tough steps regarding those individuals whose actions threaten the reservoir of trust. Leadership must act decisively to condemn the acts that have given rise to distrust, sending a message that clarifies the principles on which the organization is built.

The second challenge is to make those tough calls without creating a culture that is harsh and unforgiving. The advantages of continually upgrading talent must not be overwhelmed by competition and conflict among employees who fear they will lose their jobs.

Maintaining Systems to Share Information

High-trust organizations are information rich: people at all levels are provided with the information they need in order to fulfill their responsibilities to customers and colleagues. This information might involve, for example, the financial status of the firm, customer satisfaction levels, or competitive benchmarks of all types. In contrast, the flow of information in low-trust organizations is much more limited: vital information is often restricted to a few senior-level people. Those in other parts of the organization are not provided with the same information for fear of how they will use it. Restricted information flow corresponds to the rigid hierarchies found in organizations based on a "command and control" model. Bureaucracy institutionalizes distrust by restricting how information is shared within the organization. An employee responding to a survey noted that communication and trust must go hand in hand. For employees to buy in with management, management must be open and communicate what is expected. In contrast, "secretive management leads to employees who are unsure where they stand and unsure of their future. You can make the choice to trust each other, work together, and grow and succeed, or to take the path of adversarial relationships and fail."[14]

At Missouri's Springfield Remanufacturing Company, CEO Jack Stack opens the books to employees and provides them with time and education on the job to learn what the numbers actually mean. Each week the company shuts down the machines for half an hour while its eight hundred employees break into small groups to study the latest financial statements and review key issues or concerns. These sessions are geared toward education about and discussion of the financial performance of the firm and the actions needed to address any new problems or opportunities.[15] Says Stack, "I needed to teach anyone who moved a broom or operated a grinder everything the bank lender knows. That way they could really understand how every nickel saved could make a difference."[16] As Stack has demonstrated, information sharing and trust go hand in hand.

In contrast, a common problem in many organizations, documented by employee surveys, is a lack of direct communication, particularly among different levels in the hierarchy. No matter what the organization, direct dialogue is important if trust is to be sustained. Issues of critical importance must be dealt with in a factual manner, without any distortions or half-truths.

High-trust cultures require that people at all levels be honest and straightforward in dealing both with the business fundamentals and with the tough issues. Leaders set the tone within an organization or team regarding expectations around honest communication. Face-to-face discussions are critical to make sure people are talking about the same thing. As Packard emphasizes, "nothing beats personal, two-way communication for fostering cooperation and teamwork and for building an attitude of trust and understanding among employees."[17]

Straight talk about the business also requires effective management of differences of opinion. In cultures of trust, people are willing to offer their point of view because the goal is to develop the best approach for addressing an opportunity or threat. People in these firms will deal with differences as a natural part of the decision-making process (rather than viewing them as personal agendas among adversaries). In so doing, these high-trust groups save an enormous amount of time and energy, as issues become debates without a great deal of political maneuvering. Formal and informal mechanisms can help with this process. Senior leaders, for example, can seek to understand divergent points of view before supporting a particular course of action. They can also express discomfort when proposals reflect a lack of debate and even seek out the minority position on a particular issue.

In Motorola, each employee is entitled to file a report if others fail to support his or her ideas. These reports, called "minority reports," are read by the bosses of the employees' boss. It is considered contrary to the firm's principles to seek any retribution against those filing a minority report. Underlying this process is the understanding that personalities are less important than finding the best solution.[18] In a similar manner, some firms formalize the role of "devil's advocate" to ensure rich debate. Dataquest created a semi-formal process, called a "cat fight," to resolve in-house conflict: parties with different positions come together and work through differences in a manner designed to eliminate retribution. These meetings are structured to examine a number of action alternatives and the assumptions inherent in each. They also seek to generate new information and provide a process for reaching consensus.[19]

Instituting a Few Rigorous Strategic Controls

It would be naive to suggest that in a high-trust culture, controls are unnecessary. In reality, controls are more important in high-trust settings than in low-trust settings. Controls safeguard against abuses that would ultimately undermine the reservoir of trust within a team or organization and that could threaten the viability of the firm itself. But controls are less pervasive in high-trust settings because of the need to give individuals and teams the autonomy needed to adapt to quickly changing customer and market demands. In other words, high-trust organizations rely on fewer controls of a more strategic and critical nature.

Controls in high-trust organizations take on different forms than those found in "command and control" cultures. This is in part because high-trust organizations recognize and understand human relations. First, in high-trust organizations, most of the controls involve performance relative to outcomes rather than a myriad of operational procedures. Indeed, high-trust organizations view outcomes as the foundation for sustaining trust. For example, high-performance groups will identify a few key performance targets. These objectives, treated very seriously, are monitored to determine how well the group is doing. These "vital few" performance measures identify those who are failing to meet their targets.

Second, high-trust controls involve new approaches to organizational and team governance. In many of today's largest organizations, innovative governance structures, such as independent boards and governing bodies, are emerging and taking significant steps toward being accountable for the performance of the firms they serve. For example, the board of General Motors talked to managers several levels below the firm's senior leadership group, confirmed their worst fears about the way the company was operating, and moved to oust the CEO and his team. The revolution at GM involved a number of dramatic changes. In particular, the firm changed how its board operated, split the CEO and chairperson role, and then significantly increased the number of out-side directors.

Third, controls in high-trust organizations are often informal, in contrast to the highly restrictive control mechanisms found in low-trust firms. They may consist of reviews with supervisory and governing boards to ensure alignment on objectives and procedures. They may also consist of pressure from within oneself or informal pressure from peers to follow a firm's values and principles. For example, at Hewlett-Packard (a company of engineers), people care a great deal about their reputation in the eyes of colleagues. Those in the organization certainly recognize the potential financial benefits of success, but they also strive equally hard for the respect of their colleagues. In a highly technical firm, earning the reputation of being an "engineer's engineer" is high praise indeed.

Such monitoring is far removed from the lack of controls that allowed the Barings and Kidder Peabody scandals to occur. These firms lacked sufficient controls and placed blind faith in the good-will of employees. Since in both cases, aggressive individuals—and perhaps their supervisors—abused the autonomy they were allowed for their own financial gain, the organizations trusted too much. Strategic controls firmly in place might well have enabled the orga-nization to prevent the problems they confronted.

Fourth, controls are implemented in a manner that supports the other factors necessary to sustain a high-trust culture (such as local ownership and responsibility). In this respect, these new forms of control reinforce the need for trust rather than undermine it. As Tom Wajnert, chairman and CEO of AT&T Capital, informed me:

> In our business, controls are very important. Without them, we might quickly undermine the financial strength we need to com-pete. As a result, we have traditional audits of our operations. We try to design and implement our controls in a way that supports our philosophy of local ownership for business results. We don't want controls, as important as they are, to undermine the funda-mental way we run the business. We have established a set of norms and team processes to make the auditing process consistent with our high-trust culture.

Ultimately, the senior leader must be comfortable that appro-priate controls are in place to prevent violations of a firm's principles. This does not mean that the senior leader must personally monitor every aspect of the organization's performance. Instead, the leader must develop a limited number of strategic control mechanisms and monitor them on a periodic basis. To do anything less is to fail in one's leadership role.

✍

Reviewing the Architecture

Both employees and leaders at Hewlett-Packard clearly have the advantage of trust. I have used Hewlett-Packard in many examples throughout this book because it speaks so directly and immediately to the personal nature of high-trust organizations. Its founders set out to create the type of company that they would want to work for if they were employees. The theories and well-articulated principles came later, when Hewlett-Packard started to receive attention for its unique way of doing business.

While each organization must ultimately find its own way, the guidelines described in this chapter can help those seeking to build high-trust organizations and teams. Trust begins with the structural design of organizations and teams—that is, with the organization's architecture. Integral to that architecture are the following points:

- Aggressive business targets
- Aligned performance accountabilities
- High-ownership organizational structures
- Superior talent
- Systems to share information
- Rigorous strategic controls

Trust also hinges on the organization's culture, discussed in the next chapter. Both the architecture and the culture demand concentrated effort. And this effort is well worth it, for organizations with a reservoir of trust can more easily take actions that would otherwise meet with high levels of resistance. Whether these actions are reorganizations or the fast-paced development of new products and services, the group cohesion and flexibility they require are vital in today's marketplace.

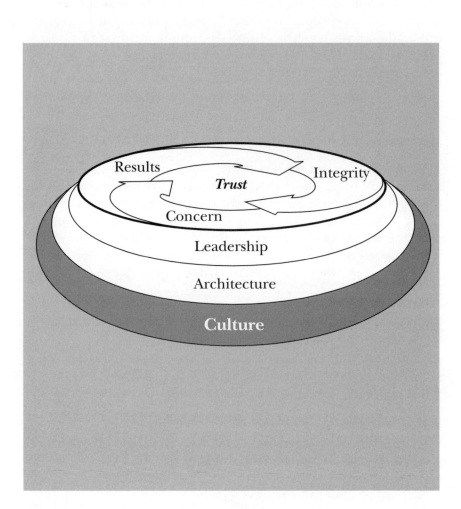

Chapter Eight

Building Trust Through Organizational Culture

Designing and implementing the formal structures and processes needed to sustain trust is a challenging task. But many business leaders believe that the hardest part of building competitive organizations and teams is managing the culture, or what is often considered the "soft side" of organizational life. They understand that values, operating principles, and norms are difficult to manage yet demand attention, for these are often key in determining how well an organization or team operates.

Indeed, these "softer" elements of the organization may demand increasing effort in the coming years. As Jack Welch of GE has said, in the 1980s it was appropriate for American companies to direct their energy "on the hardware of American business because that hardware had to be fixed. But hardware has limits." In contrast, the Japanese "have the software, the culture which ties productivity to the human spirit—which practically has no limits."[1] We must now direct our efforts to the "software" of our companies— that is, to the culture that shapes behavior.

Developing a Culture of Trust

Culture refers to those informal aspects of organizational life that have an impact on the performance of a group. As T. Ohno, the leader of Toyota, has observed, success comes not from an organization's formal systems but from the "spirit" that supports those systems. The most critical actions for developing the appropriate culture for a high-trust organization or team are

- *Develop a common vision and shared view of competitive realities.* Over time, a shared vision will enable groups to move beyond historical rivalries and be willing to take risks with one another. Recognizing external challenges or adversaries can help create a sense of shared fate.
- *Live by genuinely felt values and operating principles.* If simply stated and genuinely felt, values and operating principles can clarify expectations and promote trust.
- *Build familiarity across levels and groups.* Familiarity serves to promote understanding and concern.
- *Encourage a culture of risk taking and experimentation.* In today's environment, people must take risks and try new approaches. Methods must be in place to handle mistakes, contain them, and encourage learning from them.
- *Make visible a few powerful symbols of trust and collaboration.* Reinforce the organization's commitment to each of trust's imperatives.

Each of these actions is described in more detail in the following sections.

Developing a Common Vision and Shared View of Competitive Realities

During his tenure as CEO of Coca-Cola, Roberto Goizueta has stressed the importance of agreeing on a common view of what the organization is striving to accomplish. In particular, he believes Coke should do whatever is required to increase shareholder value. When he took charge, he stressed the fundamentals of value creation: "Nobody had taken the time to explain what our cost of capital was, that we were not reinvesting in the business, that we were paying out in dividends 60–something percent of our earnings." As Goizueta made clear, explaining that reality was critical to helping people share the vision.[2] People needed a common set of strategic assumptions; when these were in place, their expectations were less likely to diverge, and trust became more likely.

Indeed, as has been demonstrated at company after company, trust is more likely when the goals or objectives for the organization or team are clearly articulated and accepted. Often, to seek a common or similar goal, groups must move beyond historical rivalries.

This does not require that individuals have identical interests—only that they have enough in common to see a benefit in working together. Understanding what is important to others and how they view the world is critical in meeting their expectations.

In the absence of a shared vision, people question each other's motives and wonder whether others are acting out of self-interest or in the interest of the overall organization. Since trust is highly unlikely where people lack a higher-order vision that bonds them, someone must take the lead in developing and reinforcing a shared vision. It falls to the leader to help each party believe that their interests are being served through the acceptance of a shared vision; this belief enables them to take the risks required for trust to evolve.

One effective way of doing this is to find and emphasize a larger cause capable of uniting individuals in spite of the myriad differences that separate them. For this, leaders often look to the higher-order mission of the organization or team. If this mission is to capture the hearts and minds of those who must trust one another, it needs to focus on more than just earning a profit. Microsoft, for example, has a mission of fulfilling the software needs of everyone who uses a microcomputer (which, from the Microsoft view of the world, will eventually include everyone). While the company is one of the fastest-growing and most profitable firms in history, the driving force that links its people is not the creation of shareholder wealth but a shared mission with regard to the dominance of their software.

Just as people typically need a common objective in order to overcome their individual differences and trust one another, many also need an external competitor on whom to focus. The leader can choose to emphasize a "worthy competitor" to bring home the importance of acting in concert to achieve the common goals. This can result in higher levels of internal cohesion and trust. But the leader must choose an external threat that is worthy of people's attention. It need not be the largest firm in a particular industry— but it must be notable for important reasons. For example, most American firms in the automotive industry now use Toyota, which is significantly smaller than GM, as the target for their efforts to improve the quality and cost of their vehicles.

The external referent can be a firm (consider, for example, Cannon's motto of "Beat Xerox," Pepsi's of "Overtake Coke,"

Komatsu's of "Encircle Caterpillar," and MCI's of "Attack AT&T"); it can be an industry group (in which case the motto might be "We want to be the best firm in our industry in these three key areas"); or it can be a competitive benchmark ("We want to win the Baldridge despite tough competition for the award").

Welch, of GE, and Goizueta, of Coke, addressed the idea of an external adversary in an interview recently published in *Fortune*:

Welch: We compete with giants. So we have an enemy, if you will. We compete with companies and governments.

Goizueta: That's great. If you don't have an enemy, the best thing you can do is create one.

Welch: You have to have one. . . . You have to rally around a benchmark. . . . Take a look at what a refrigerator cost fifteen years ago, and take a look at what an automobile cost fifteen years ago. A refrigerator sells for just about the same price as fifteen years ago. An automobile, two and a half times, or whatever it is. We've had to fight in competitive industries like that every day and grow margins and grow returns. Our price index for the last seven years is probably negative as a company, yet our profits have grown at double-digit rates. That comes from using capital more efficiently, using people more efficiently, from systems behavior.[3]

Some leaders, often with reputations as turnaround artists, create an adversary soon after taking charge of a firm. Their intent is to get people to stop dwelling on their differences and unite to defeat a common enemy. In this way, any tendency for people to mistrust each other is redirected away from people within the organization to the external threat (or opportunity).

Such use of "external threats" is not without its risks. It may simply shift attention away from the real problems inside an organization. Or it may result in a culture that seeks scapegoats, internal as well as external, for any problems. Leaders who set up external adversaries must therefore understand the potential for backlash and even higher levels of suspicion.

Motorola offers a positive example of how to use an external threat to align people within organizations and teams. In the early

1980s, Motorola's leadership was beginning to sense that the rapid growth of the previous decade was masking fundamental quality problems. Robert Galvin, as CEO, began to highlight the growing superiority of other global electronics conglomerates. To avoid a slow annihilation, he decided that Motorola needed to make its products much better and much cheaper. He moved from targeting a few foreign competitors to the key quality and speed measures on which he would focus the organization. People, often within functions that had a history of competing with each other, now were required to work collaboratively if the organization was going to reach its extremely aggressive goals. And as Motorola's success attests, they have collaborated well.

Living by Genuinely Felt Values and Operating Principles

Trust is more likely when people share a common set of general principles and norms. In many professions, norms of various types guide the behavior of members. Trust is enhanced because we assume that these members have internalized an established set of norms and thus can be relied on to behave in a manner consistent with our expectations. The Hippocratic oath encapsulates a type of norm-guided behavior within the medical field, for example. The existence of the oath does not mean that all medical doctors abide by its precepts, nor does it eliminate malpractice. But it does suggest that we can expect a certain kind of behavior from those on whom we depend—and it provides a yardstick by which we can measure how well individuals are living up to these expectations.

As a general rule, trust arises when people share a set of values so that certain expectations about consistent and honest behavior exist. To some extent, the particular character of the values is less important than the fact that they are shared.[4]

Relationships in business are far too complex to be completely covered by written agreements or in-depth contingency plans. Consequently, trust requires a set of overall values and norms that can guide the behavior of individuals and teams. Each organization needs to develop and reinforce a set of "trust-sustaining" norms— what Nietzsche referred to as the "language of good and evil." For example, at Pepsi there is a deeply felt belief in the importance of results and integrity.[5] These terms have a specific meaning in the

Pepsi culture that people come to learn as a result of their experience in the corporation. *Results* involve making a difference in the company and delivering the outcomes you promise. *Integrity* involves complete openness and honesty, as well as fulfilling your commitments to others. Results and integrity are just two words, but they carry a great deal of power in the Pepsi culture. Within Pepsi, it is assumed that those who rise to positions of leadership can be relied on to deliver results and act with integrity—and thus can be trusted to use the firm's resources in the best interests of the customers, shareholders, and employees. As a result, Pepsi's executives have a great deal of leeway in how they run their businesses or groups.

Craig Weatherup, Pepsi-Cola's chair, recalled an incident during Roger Enrico's tenure as Pepsi's CEO that demonstrated values in action:

> We were off target by $20 million in Pepsi USA, and in those days that was a big number. I went in and said, "I hate to give you the news but the reality is we're going to miss plan by twenty million bucks." He earned his stripes with me that day because although he was more than a little upset, he listened intently so he could understand why and immediately sought to help me solve the problem and make the best of a bad situation. It was a great illustration of Pepsi at its best and a great example of leadership. I didn't sugarcoat the news, and he handled it perfectly. That's what builds trust in leadership.

Welch, at GE, also believes in the power of a few simple values to bind people together and drive performance. In many respects, the values and operating principles of an organization articulate the rights *and* duties of individuals within the firm. They make more explicit the expectations that come with being a member of the organization. Welch comments on what sets his company apart:

> The success of our company lies in the fact that a lot of people understand these values. They have joined the company knowing these were the values, and they work to implement them. This is our life. This is how we behave. If someone cheats in our company, they're thrown out the first time. If somebody's boundary or turf oriented, they get a second chance, but they don't get a third. If

they're not open, if they don't share ideas, that's bad behavior. We're translating values into operational behavior.[6]

People at all levels need to behave in a way that is consistent with the espoused values of the organization, but this is especially true at the leadership level. A leader who acts as if people are simply a means to an end will undermine the values of a firm that believes in respect for the individual. The senior leader, therefore, must take great pains to ensure that the top leadership cadre—the top one hundred to one thousand people—lives within the parameters of the firm's accepted values and operating principles. Some senior leaders, for example, will interview candidates for positions several levels below in order to sense the fit with the values they hold to be important. They will also conduct reviews of the top one hundred to five hundred people to ensure that those being promoted to higher levels have the attributes and values needed to sustain the firm's culture. Others will take action to remove those who violate the firm's norms, particularly those that relate to how the firm's employees are treated. The key, in these examples, is the investment of time to ensure that the values are understood and demonstrated by the senior leadership of the firm.

Building Familiarity Across Levels and Groups

Charles Handy has noted that you can't trust those you don't see.[7] It is equally true that it is hard to trust those you don't know. In most cases, distrust increases in proportion to our lack of familiarity with those on whom we depend. At the simplest level, trust requires some real or perceived access to others, which allows us to determine if we have a common agenda or shared values and norms. Familiarity also allows us to determine if others are capable of delivering results and if they are concerned about the well-being of others. In the absence of familiarity, many people begin to distrust. The paradox of trust is that as technology increasingly allows us to work with others sight unseen, it becomes more important to meet face to face.

Tom Wajnert of AT&T Capital believes trust is founded on direct contact and interaction between leadership and members of the organization. Here is how he described it in our interview:

Visibility is very important in establishing a sense of trust. I made a commitment as the CEO to spend time with every member of the organization on a regular basis—which is tough when you have a firm of 2,800 people. But I have done it over the past few years and will continue to remain as accessible as possible. We have breakfast meetings with our members once a month. They are invited to join us for an informal discussion about our business and our future direction. These meetings have worked very well in terms of the senior strategic team getting to know others and, in turn, their learning more about us.

As Wajnert has learned and taken to heart, trust is more likely when people believe they can be on familiar terms with those in positions of power and when they feel they have a voice in how the business can and should improve. Given the need for senior leadership to focus on a variety of external stakeholders (including, among others, key customers, board members, industry groups, financial analysts, and members of the press), there is often limited time for interaction with organizational members. The risk, however, is that these members will then view leadership as detached from the organization, and this view is likely to increase feelings of distrust about the senior leadership. Some leaders, like George Fisher of Eastman Kodak, make a point of meeting with employees in order to stay in touch. Almost every day, Fisher has breakfast in the company cafeteria with employees. He also invites anyone with a question or concern to send him e-mail, which he personally answers.[8]

In contrast, the executive team of one large company with which I have worked rarely left the tenth floor of the corporate headquarters building. These team members ate in an executive dining suite and entered and exited the building via a private entry and elevator. The few times they would interact with employees were during special holidays or company events. On these occasions, they were stiff and formal. Over time, they came to be seen as out of touch with the organization (which they were) and relatively unconcerned about the welfare of the firm's employees (which was also true).

As another example, consider the research group of a large multinational corporation. The staff of the research group was located thousands of miles away from the senior leadership of the corporation. This was done by design in order to encourage more creative approaches to the business. The research group was also distant from the marketing managers who needed to understand the innovative products that were coming out of the research facility. While a myriad of factors complicated the relationship among these groups, the lack of familiarity only exacerbated the differences that already existed. The groups would come into contact only when important decisions needed to be made. As might be predicted, the result was mistrust and, over time, a poor track record bringing new products to market.

Approaches to developing familiarity include limiting the size of organizations within a company, locating key groups together, and using small teams whenever possible. A few examples follow:

- ABB, the large engineering concern, organizes itself into thousands of small business units. This is done, in part, to maintain a sense of shared understanding and cohesion.
- W. L. Gore and Associates, the $1 billion maker of Gore-Tex, regards 150 to 200 people as roughly the optimal size for the manufacturing organizations that populate their "lattice organization."
- As noted earlier, Hewlett-Packard and Johnson & Johnson have for decades created relatively small, independent divisions where familiarity is possible.

Hewlett-Packard has institutionalized a number of management techniques to ensure regular and ongoing contact among people at all levels. These include having executive offices in the plant or service areas, an "open-door policy" where skip-level conversations are possible, and regular contact between leaders and members of the organization. This policy is designed to build mutual trust and understanding and to create an environment in which people feel free to express their ideas, opinions, problems, and concerns.[9]

Providing access to people across groups and levels builds familiarity and is particularly important as the demands of global businesses increase and people have less time to interact. As Bill Raduchel of Sun Microsystems notes, "you can't have a virtual conversation unless you also have real conversations. The indispensable complementary technology to the net is the Boeing 747."[10]

Organizations must take actions to strengthen people's personal connections in an age where technology makes these connections less likely.

Encouraging a Culture of Risk Taking and Experimentation

The importance of a bias in favor of action is evident when we consider the extreme opposite: a highly rigid and inflexible structure where actions are taken only as a last resort. In these settings, people can come to believe that the organization or team as a whole is ill prepared to deal with a rapidly changing business environment and unwilling to trust people to meet competitive pressures.

In a business setting, the ability to make decisions quickly and move forward with initiatives is key in sustaining trust. Steve Kerr, vice president of corporate management development at GE, believes that a bias for action is needed for trust to develop in an organization. In Kerr's experience, the Workout! process, where unnecessary work is eliminated from the business, helped to support a bias for action by stressing the need for quick decisions and concrete wins. It enabled people to see the results of their efforts incrementally. Kerr recalled one Workout! session in which "people were focusing on what I thought were rather trivial administrative matters. They moved forward on those items, came to trust the process was in fact going to make a difference, and then moved on to tougher issues." In other words, once the participants saw that they could achieve results by taking action on the smaller issues, they were able to tackle the larger ones. As Kerr said, at GE, "we trust people and let them put the ball into play." Without that trust—and with a great deal of discussion and very little action instead—Kerr believes "people will quickly become cynical." People need to see that a real difference will be made as a result of their efforts.

A bias for action, for encouraging people to act decisively, inevitably results in a significant number of mistakes. Firms that set high performance objectives, move fast, and take risks understand that failures will occur. The key, in relation to trust, is to develop approaches that ensure both that these failures will not threaten the firm's survival and that people will learn from these experiences and thus decrease the likelihood of making the same mistakes again. Each firm, therefore, should develop formal or informal approaches to dealing with situations of crisis, including rules of escalation, which dictate when and how issues are brought to the surface with others in the organization. In well-designed firms, people understand when a situation is beyond what can be handled using normal procedures. They then invoke more detailed procedures or involve others in analyzing and resolving the problem. For example, in the financial services industry a host of controls indicates when the firm is exposing itself to excessive risk. Some firms understand the risks and move quickly to determine the appropriate course of action. Otherwise, an organization may make mistakes of a magnitude that would stifle further innovation and bold action—as we have seen recently in firms such as Diawa. There, one trader, who had nearly complete freedom, cost his firm over a billion dollars in losses.

Once mechanisms are in place to contain the downside of taking risks, a culture that allows people to deal more effectively with failure is necessary. The founders of AES Corporation, a power producer that sells electricity to utilities, developed a positive and effective approach to failure. In this company's culture, failure—and the need for people not to be overwhelmed by it—are seen as inevitable parts of the business equation. For this reason, the founders crafted a value statement that emphasizes the importance of fun. But as they note, "we're not talking about Friday afternoon beer busts. Fun is when you are intellectually excited and you are interacting with each other. . . . It's the struggle, and the failures that go with it, that make work fun."[11] In the AES organization, employees are given a great deal of autonomy to run various aspects of the business. And in contrast to most firms, there is trust that those who fail will be given an opportunity to learn from their mistakes and become better at their jobs as a result. The positive aspects of failure, including evidence of having taken risks, are acknowledged.

Like AES, other high-trust organizations give people the freedom to fail and then deal effectively with failure when it occurs. The ability to get through difficult times, to support people when they are vulnerable, can build trust as much as anything else does. Consider, for example, the success of 3M in fostering innovation over its history. The firm has met a well-known objective of bringing in 25 percent of its total revenue from products introduced within the last five-year period. It is also recognized for providing its researchers with up to 15 percent of their time to work on projects that they personally deem important, without formal authorization from supervisors. One of the firm's most influential leaders during its growth period, William McKnight, noted that 3M has a culture that accepts "well-intentioned failure." As he has said, "management that is destructively critical when mistakes are made kills initiative," and this initiative is essential for growth. In the long run, if people are essentially right, their mistakes are not as serious as the mistakes that management will make "if it is dictatorial and undertakes to tell those under its authority exactly how they must do their job."[12]

Making Visible a Few Powerful Symbols of Trust

Most companies that have developed high-trust cultures have a rich assortment of stories or artifacts that reflect the need for trust. Hewlett-Packard, for example, is replete with stories about the firm's founders that speak to this need. Packard was well aware of the problems that can be caused when a company lacks trust in its people. When he worked for General Electric in Schenectady in the late 1930s, plant security had top priority. GE was particularly careful to guard the tool and parts bins so that employees couldn't steal anything. But this obvious display of distrust sparked many employees to test security by walking off with tools or parts. As Packard reported, the irony was that many employees were then using their lifted tools and parts "to work on either job-related projects or skill-enhancing hobbies—activities that would likely improve their performance on the job." When Packard was starting his new company, these memories motivated him to keep parts bins and storerooms open. This simple act offered two important advantages to HP. On the practical side, the ready availability of parts and tools "helped product designers and others who wanted to work out new ideas at home or on the weekends." A second, less tangible but no less important benefit was that the open bins and storerooms became "a symbol of trust, a trust that is central to the way Hewlett-Packard does business."[13]

Beyond open access to tools and parts, Hewlett-Packard has developed a myriad of other "trust symbols." One is the practice of engineers leaving everything they are working on out on their desktops so that others can understand their work and, more important, make suggestions for improvement. The open books at SRC provide yet another powerful—and company-wide—symbol of trust.

✑

Shaping the Culture of Trust

The actions described in this chapter as ways to shape an organization's culture in order to build and sustain trust suggest what is possible. Certainly one could come up with additional ways to encourage and support trust, but these offer a starting point:

- Common vision and shared view of competitive realities
- Core set of genuinely felt values and operating principles
- Familiarity across organizational levels and groups
- Culture of risk taking and experimentation
- Visible symbols of trust and collaboration

The key point is that leaders should spend sufficient time understanding and influencing the direction of their firm's informal culture. It is also important to note that culture is usually impacted indirectly—through finding creative ways to address such fundamental business issues as the firm's competitive standing or the need to surpass an adversary in the marketplace.

As we've seen in the chapters in Part Three, trust requires skill in managing both the architecture and culture of organizational life. In the final part of this book, the dilemmas of trust take center stage.

Trust Lost,
Trust Regained

Part Four addresses the critical dilemmas associated with trust. In particular, I explore the inevitable conflicts that arise among the three trust imperatives (achieving results, acting with integrity, and demonstrating concern). I examine the role of leadership in balancing these tradeoffs. In this section, I also examine cases of low trust and the actions required to a create a more positive work environment.

In the three chapters of this section, I highlight several key themes:

1. Trust requires a sufficient level of performance on each of the three imperatives. Extremely low levels on one of the imperatives (results, integrity, or concern) can overwhelm higher levels on the other two. Leaders and organizations must be aware of the consequences of failing to meet the threshold requirements in any one area. Achieving just "two out of three" of the trust imperatives is usually not enough to sustain trust.

2. Low-trust environments are extremely difficult to change. Distrust is typically self-sustaining and resistant to improvement (even in the face of positive information or events). Most efforts to address suspicion are inadequate. As a result, those seeking to overcome high levels of distrust must take extreme measures—and realize that change will not occur quickly.

3. Trust is best addressed by dealing with the factors that give rise to it (rather than through talking about trust's importance and

the actions one is taking to sustain it). Trust is the outcome of doing a number of fundamental things right. Those who are successful at building trust usually don't talk about it; they live it.

Chapters Nine, Ten, and Eleven look at specific challenges associated with trust and offer advice for dealing with its basic dilemmas.

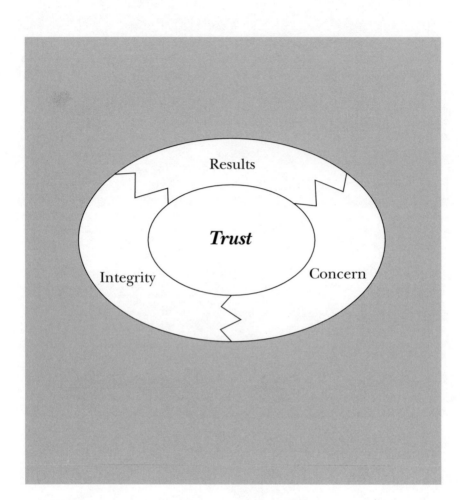

Chapter Nine

Managing the Dilemmas of Trust

In this book, I suggest that trust is based on three imperatives: results, integrity, and concern. I also suggest that the most important leverage points in building trust are leadership and the design of organizations (including a firm's formal architecture and its informal culture). In this chapter, the focus shifts to common dilemmas that can quickly erode trust if not managed effectively. These dilemmas are particularly important because trust is like a ratchet that turns easily in one direction but not in the other; in other words, trust can be broken more easily than it can be built up again.[1] The situations discussed in this chapter often determine whether trust will be won or lost.

Building trust requires more than establishing an appropriate organizational structure or set of values. It rests on the ability of a firm and its leaders to manage effectively a few central dilemmas. I use the term *dilemma* to suggest a predicament that cannot be easily resolved—a situation in which two forces, both of which we value, are in conflict. For example, leaders in many firms want to cut costs while increasing revenues. Both goals are important in today's world, yet they are often in conflict. Those firms that simply cut costs without finding new revenue will most likely fail—as will those that simply increase revenue without paying attention to cost and profitability.

Dilemmas, in contrast to problems, cannot be resolved completely but rather only dealt with in effective or ineffective ways. A problem is simpler: if a mistake is made, we can act to correct it. A dilemma is often made worse if we treat it like a problem.[2]

Trying to resolve what cannot be resolved results in denial of the predicament, which will not go away, and associated missteps.

One way of understanding the dilemmas of trust is to consider the tradeoffs among the three trust imperatives—achieving results, acting with integrity, and demonstrating concern. As earlier chapters in this book suggest, each of these imperatives can be in conflict with the others. For example, delivering profits in a highly competitive business environment is a challenge in itself. To do so in a way that demonstrates concern is even more difficult. Thus, the dilemma: how do you achieve results while demonstrating concern? Why can't we just focus on results and not worry about demonstrating concern? Or why can't we just treat our people well and not worry about results? The answer, of course, is that both are required to sustain high performance—and high trust.

Integrity, which can be viewed as the degree of consistency or coherence in a firm's strategy or a leader's behavior, is necessary as well. In fact, one can argue that results can be achieved over the long term only through integrity. This argument is made by firms as well respected as Pepsi, General Electric, and Hewlett-Packard. While ethical violations occur in every large firm, an ongoing pattern suggesting a lack of ethical integrity will eventually erode the confidence of both employees and customers. Yet in the face of competitive pressures, organizations and their leaders must in some cases change directions and tactics rapidly. If they do so repeatedly, leadership will be seen as being inconsistent and, perhaps, incompetent.

Sustaining an appropriate balance among results, integrity, and concern is difficult within any organization or team. The dilemmas and tradeoffs discussed in this chapter fall into the following categories: strategic mistakes, ethical violations, "brute force" management, corporate downsizing, and reengineering. These dilemmas present special cases where the conflicts among the imperatives of trust become even more pronounced.

Strategic Mistakes

In today's highly competitive world, mistakes are inevitable. They occur as businesses seek new competitive advantage and, in doing so, take risks that were unnecessary even ten or twenty years ago.

Mistakes are more likely in today's environment—and can be more costly than in years past. Mistakes are also likely to be more visible, since the business press has grown and become more aggressive in its reporting.

Big mistakes can erode confidence in an organization and call into question the belief that an organization and its members will remain competitive. They can also undermine the credibility of those leading the organization. Roger Smith was distrusted by many of his employees and eventually his board because of the mistakes he made in positioning General Motors to compete in the 1990s. For example, Smith invested billions in technology intended to dramatically improve GM's productivity, but he had little to show in the way of results. Similarly, in the late 1980s, CEO John Ackers lost the confidence of many IBM employees due to the steady decline of IBM's revenues and market share. More recently, CEO Bob Allen of AT&T has come under fire for his missteps in acquiring NCR. He may, like John Reed at Citibank, recover and regain the full confidence of his employees and external stakeholders. Or he may retire over the next few years with a reputation for having failed to build on the legacy he inherited when he took over AT&T.

Highly visible mistakes cause people to question whether the organization and its leaders can achieve results—one of the imperatives for trust. In this case, the dilemma is achieving predicable results in a world where mistakes are inevitable and are part of the price of doing business. In situations in which strategic errors have eroded confidence in an organization's ability to prosper or in a leader's ability to lead, several steps are helpful. Simply put, these are to own the problem, extract learning from the situation, enforce accountability, and demonstrate progress.

Taking Responsibility for the Problem

Suspicion increases when those responsible for mistakes are seen putting a positive "spin" on the situation (in an attempt to portray failure as something closer to success). Suspicion is also likely when people distance themselves from the negative outcomes of their actions (in an attempt to show that they are not responsible for the mistakes that were made). Many believed, for example that Ackers did not hold himself or his leadership team fully accountable for the problems facing IBM. Building trust requires that those responsible for the errors admit them and, as necessary, explain the factors that produced the failure. This does not need to be a protracted process, but it must be visible enough so that people recognize that those involved have taken responsibility for their actions. Goizueta, CEO of Coca-Cola, took complete responsibility for the failed introduction of New Coke and acted quickly to correct it.

Extracting Learning from Failures

In addition to taking responsibility for the problem, Goizueta took the next step and found the lesson in failure. He has observed that New Coke's failed introduction was a turning point for him in recognizing the importance of the Coke brand in the minds of the company's customers.[3]

In contrast, many leaders attempt to deny that they have made a mistake. They treat failures as embarrassments that are best quickly forgotten—for all concerned. Often, a few people are scapegoated, allowing others to wash their hands of the whole episode. The obvious problem with this approach is that the organization fails to learn from its mistakes. The firm has paid the price but gained only limited insight. As a result, people become suspicious; they realize that leaders are sacrificing the truth in order to avoid the discomfort associated with failure.

Trust requires that failures be openly discussed, fully understood, and as appropriate, communicated to people throughout the organization. Both formal mechanisms and informal norms are needed to ensure that this occurs. An illustration of this approach can be found in the early introductions of Japanese automobiles to the United States. Nissan, Honda, and Toyota all introduced products that were inferior—to the point that many people found them comical. The Japanese, however, extracted lessons from their failures and over time developed vehicles that have far surpassed all others in quality and cost. One GM executive, who had worked in joint ventures with the Japanese in Fremont, California, in the 1980s, put it this way: "at GM we are literally applauded for being able to cover over problems. In contrast, at Fremont they made them heroes when they stopped the line or pointed out an inconsistency or discrepancy. You can't understand the significance of this change until you have worked in both worlds."[4]

Enforcing Accountability Across All Levels

Suspicion is to be expected when a double standard exists within an organization. In some firms, employees believe that senior leadership is rarely held accountable for its mistakes. Similarly, certain organizational groups can become "sacred cows" and be—or appear to be—immune from the consequences of their failures. In many organizations, for example, corporate staff groups are held to a lower performance standard than that applied to field operations. Trust requires that people at all levels and in all groups be held accountable for their mistakes. This does not necessarily mean that they should be punished or fired. The consequences for failure will vary depending on the severity of the mistake and the culture of the company. In some cases, those who made the mistake should be removed from their jobs. In other cases, they could be moved to new positions that better fit their skills. And in still other situations, they might remain in their current positions but be asked to learn from their mistakes and address the problems that have surfaced. The intent is to be fair in seeking to understand the causes of the problems and equitable in dealing with those involved.

Demonstrating Progress

Ultimately, trust is recovered after strategic mistakes by taking decisive actions that move an organization or team forward. In many cases, this involves bringing in a new cadre of senior leaders who represent a new approach (as we have seen over the past decade at IBM, GM, and Kodak). While new leadership is not always necessary, in many cases those responsible for the mistakes cannot move beyond them. This may be because the leaders refuse to learn from their failures and adopt bold new practices. Others may recognize the need for change but cannot shed the perception that they are responsible for a firm's problems. Or consider the example of the recent turmoil at Apple Computer and Michael Spindler's unwillingness to accept responsibility for his firm's problems. He was unable to chart a clear course of action to correct the significant challenges that Apple faced. Apple's board finally concluded that Spindler, whatever his strengths, did not have a viable plan—or the internal or external backing—required for him to lead the company effectively. Apple needed a leader who was capable of taking charge and establishing a new course of action to prove that the business can recover and grow. The board brought in Gil Amelio to replace Spindler. He has developed a concrete plan and taken some initial steps to simplify Apple's product line, cut unprofitable businesses (such as the firm's Internet service), and reduce costs. Actions such as these are often easier for those who have no responsibility for past decisions and the failures associated with them. Amelio will have a brief window of time in which to demonstrate that he can make a difference in overcoming the mistakes of his predecessors.

The goal for leadership is to restore confidence through actions that indicate the organization is willing to do what is required to move forward. Consider the recent turnaround at Continental. After being with the firm for one year, Gordon Bethune became CEO and quickly put together what he and his team called the "Go Forward" plan, consisting of key strategies to restore Continental's profitability (and described in more detail in Chapter Ten). In this case, a clear, concise plan was quickly implemented in order to show immediate progress.

The speed was vital. Employees had seen many different plans introduced over the years by new management teams with little or no impact. They were cynical and in no mood to support yet another set of corporate initiatives. Bethune and his team needed to show results—and fast. They did: within a year Continental had earned back its profitability and the trust of a workforce that had lost faith in both the leadership and the organization.

Ethical Violations

As with strategic mistakes, ethical violations can erode trust within an organization or team. This is particularly true in relation to those in leadership positions. The dilemma is that organizations can't compete if too many controls are in place; people need the autonomy to act quickly and with few restrictions.

Some people feel that the need for results conflicts with the need for consistency and integrity. Dealing with this dilemma, therefore, requires a necessary and ongoing balance between complete employee autonomy (in the name of results) and complete control of employees (in the name of consistency). Several of GE's employees, for example, have violated the firm's standards of integrity in striving to achieve outstanding financial results and for personal gain. A recent visible example occurred in what was GE's investment group, where a trader was charged with engaging in fraudulent practices. GE has put into place new controls where needed but has not changed the fundamental principle that gives people within the firm a great deal of autonomy in pursuing business objectives.

General Electric now uses a simple leadership model to help explain the necessary balance between results and values. A recent GE annual report states that

> In our view, leaders, whether on the shop floor or at the tops of our businesses, can be characterized in at least four ways.
>
> - The first is one who delivers on commitments—financial or otherwise—and shares the values of our Company. His or her future is an easy call. Onward and upward.
>
> - The second type of leader is one who does not meet commitments and does not share our values. Not as pleasant a call, but equally easy.
>
> - The third is one who misses commitments but shares the values. He or she usually gets a second chance, preferably in a different environment.
>
> - Then there's the fourth type—the most difficult for many of us to deal with. That leader delivers on commitments, makes all the numbers, but doesn't share the values we must have. This is the person who typically forces performance out of people rather than inspires it: the autocrat, the big shot, the tyrant. Too often all of us have looked the other way—tolerated these "Type 4" managers because "they always deliver"—at least in the short-term.[5]

How GE responds to its "Type 4" managers is key. It must clearly take action on these leaders, through developmental efforts or removal, if this approach to leadership is to be more than simple rhetoric.

As Jack Welch describes it, "no one at GE loses a job because of a missed quarter . . . a missed year . . . or a mistake. That's nonsense and everyone knows it. A company would be paralyzed in an atmosphere like that. People get second chances. Many get thirds and fourths, along with training, help, even different jobs. There is only one performance failure where there is no second chance. That's a clear integrity violation. If you commit one of those, you're out."[6]

Leaders acting in a deceptive or immoral way will erode their own credibility and, over time, the confidence that people have in the organization as a whole. Consider, for example, recent events at Bausch & Lomb. The firm's former CEO, Daniel E. Gill, had created a "performance at all costs" environment. This resulted in false financial reporting and a host of other unethical business practices. In the early 1990s, Bausch & Lomb's managers felt pushed by Gill's demands for double-digit annual profit growth. In their attempts to meet those demands, they would take the expedient path—often in lieu of ethical business practices. For example, they gave customers "extraordinarily long payment terms, knowingly fed gray markets [that undercut the sales of regular customers], and threatened to cut off distributors unless they took on huge quantities of unwanted products."[7] Some managers even took it a step further by shipping product even before customers placed an order. The company is also alleged to have indirectly aided money laundering through lucrative Latin American sales.

Not surprisingly, B&L's performance-oriented ethos produced stellar results for many years. But in the early 1990s, B&L's markets slowed just as several acquisitions soured, and the company's culture was a "train wreck" waiting to happen. A plunge in profitability finally took place in 1993 and 1994, when B&L maintained its steep growth targets even as markets stalled.[8] The various violations of standard business practices came to the surface, and the firm's CEO was forced to resign.

Taking Immediate Action

Trust requires that violators of group standards be dealt with swiftly. Trust has a tough side that demands fair but harsh treatment of those who are dishonest, who steal from the firm or its clients or in other ways act unethically. Violations of this type are more than an individual affair; they impact the reputation and culture within an organization and must be addressed with speed and conviction. At

Bausch & Lomb, for example, there was evidence, in some cases only secondhand, that Gill's insistence on results at all costs was driving people to unethical behaviors and business practices. Had the board intervened earlier and sought to confirm their suspicions, the subsequent problems might have been averted. The firm's superior financial results, however, made such scrutiny unlikely.

Conducting an Organizational Audit

Rarely are individuals' actions completely independent of a larger set of cultural norms and practices. Thus, violations of ethical standards may indicate that an organization's culture is motivating people to act unethically. In the most benign cases, a lack of discussion about ethical standards can produce a culture of tolerance that is inappropriate in a few key areas. In more extreme cases, the firm can create pressures that produce objectionable behavior—as occurred at B&L. The pressure to deliver bottom-line results can become so intense that people distort financial results. An unethical or purely profit-driven culture can also motivate people to ship products that are defective or not fit for the purpose intended.

It is critical to look at the larger organization and assess to what degree its culture and management practices have influenced the actions of the individuals or groups caught violating standards. The audit should examine the entire scope of the firm (including leadership, structure, performance expectations, and rewards); it should have a particular emphasis on the informal culture and the pressure it places on people. For example, some organizations create extremely high performance standards and follow through with significant rewards for those who perform and negative consequences for those who don't. These same firms may also provide a great deal of autonomy to both individuals and teams. This combination of factors, in the absence of strong norms around appropriate behavior, will often produce ethical violations.

Establishing Appropriate Safeguards

Having conducted an audit and found parts of the organizational culture lacking, leaders can put safeguards into place to prevent future ethical violations. This, of course, must be done in a way that

still allows people the autonomy needed to meet the business challenges they face. In particular, firms must be careful that they
don't, in the name of control, create a myriad of bureaucratic policies that frustrate everyone and harm performance. When it is
clear that more and better controls are needed, these should be
designed and instituted in a way that retains the best of the current
culture. These controls may consist of formal policies and systems
or informal norms. The goal is to create both formal and informal
mechanisms that discourage violations while allowing any that do
occur to come to the surface.

Brute Force Management

Many large organizations have a history of delivering results. But in
some of these firms, there is little concern for employees. When the
drive to achieve results overwhelms any perceived need to demonstrate concern, employees come to believe that they are simply a
means to an end—that they have little or no value to the firm beyond
what can be extracted from them. As one employee noted, "cutthroat
business people want quality and production, and if you can't give
them what they want, they'll find someone who can."[9] In extreme situations, employees feel taken advantage of, even abused, and become
highly suspicious of the organization and its leadership. In these
cases, behavior contradictory to a larger set of values and principles
is tolerated as long as people deliver results. In less extreme cases,
employees believe that the organization is not really concerned about
them as people or as employees, despite rhetoric to the contrary.

Consider the firm where a drive for results begins to overwhelm
its regard for people. In these organizations, no one feels safe. Mistakes are viewed as unacceptable. Those who offend the most powerful fear the loss of their jobs. Problems are hidden, and ownership
for problems beyond one's own area of responsibility is rare. Teams
within the organization are more likely to compete than cooperate.
One sign that this type of culture exists is a wave of executive depar-
tures (and difficulty attracting talented new people). High turnover
is common in cultures where this quarter's results are the only thing
that matters. People are expendable when leadership seeks results
at any cost. People will also leave of their own accord when given
an opportunity to work in a more supportive environment.

Another consequence of a mentality that focuses on results at any cost is the suppression of individual initiative and creativity. In these organizations, those who remain often strive to meet the expectations of the senior leadership group by following what they believe to be acceptable operating procedures. Fearing failure, they will at least try to act in a way that fits the preferences of those demanding results. Ironically, their desire to please can undermine the creativity and individual initiative needed to deliver business results over the long term.

A number of steps can be taken to deal with the distrust evident when a "brute force" mentality has permeated an organization. These include acting on values and operating principles, developing a culture in which people matter, and stressing development and growth.

Acting on Values and Operating Principles

A drive for results must be balanced with a more general set of principles and values around how people should operate within a firm or team. This does not mean that every contingency must be spelled out. Core principles on the human side of the business, however, are important. These include standards of integrity and honesty, teamwork, and mutual support. Each firm will describe their values in unique language; the emphasis will vary depending on the firm's history and competitive environment. But no matter what an organization's history, the key is to articulate these values and then establish processes to ensure that they are acted on.

Developing a Culture Where People Matter

Those firms wishing to move beyond a "brute force" mentality should establish a number of formal and informal practices that underscore the importance of organizational members. These practices should be consistently linked to the business challenges facing the firm (in contrast to add-on initiatives that may be potentially effective but become unnecessary overhead).

Hewlett-Packard may be the most visible example of a firm that strives to deliver hard results through the development of a culture that values people (see Chapter Seven). Most important, HP tries to eliminate any practice that undermines its culture of support. An example of this type of linked effort is found in HP's willingness to give employees flexibility in their work schedules. This policy gives employees another tool to help them balance the competing demands of work and home. The benefit to the company is that employees can perform more effectively and with fewer distractions while on the job.

Stressing Development and Growth

Perhaps the most important place where the needs of individuals and the needs of the firm converge is in the area of professional development. Emphasizing the importance of development can go a long way to assuring people that their firm is concerned about them. Of course, this should not be accomplished in a paternalistic way, in which the firm takes charge of and assumes responsibility for the employees' development. Instead, each member of the organization should become primarily responsible for identifying and acting on developmental opportunities. The firm, in turn, is responsible for providing the opportunities and supporting the employee's initiative in this area.

Downsizing

Perhaps no other single factor has had as dramatic an impact on the erosion of trust in corporate America as the massive downsizing of the past decade. Most large U.S. firms have significantly reduced their workforces. Indeed, the downsizings have reached such significant levels that politicians are threatening governmental action unless the reductions become less extreme.

In downsizing situations, employees often become cynical and withdrawn. This attitude develops just when the successful transition through a period of change depends on people remaining open to new ways of operating. Yet is it surprising that distrust is likely when people find themselves in a constantly changing and uncertain environment? Is it surprising that people are distrustful when their associates are losing their jobs while their firms earn record profits? Is it surprising that distrust becomes more prevalent when people see their compensation and benefits being reduced while senior leadership is richly rewarded?

The dilemma is that firms must become more productive in order to compete, yet in doing so, they erode the collective sense of ownership and cohesion that is needed to compete over the long term. Consider, for example, the impact of downsizing on the three imperatives for trust.

Downsizing and Achieving Results

Workforce reductions are typically designed to improve a firm's productivity and ultimately, its financial performance. Yet in many cases, reductions in a firm's workforce come about because of strategic or operational failures. In this respect, downsizing calls into question the capability of a firm's leadership and, more specifically, the degree to which employees should place their trust in them. Apple Computer's recent reductions in staff, for example, were in large part due to critical mistakes and missteps made by the organization that pushed the firm to the brink of collapse. To suggest that Apple's problems reflect the turbulence of the computer industry is to ignore the successes of some of its competitors. While Apple has stumbled, Hewlett-Packard, Dell, and Compaq have significantly increased their revenues.

In another field, Bob Allen is currently under criticism for his announcement that forty thousand people will lose their jobs at AT&T. Some are blaming Allen's decision to buy NCR as one of the factors that led to the layoffs. An article in the *Wall Street Journal* notes:

> Instead of a coolly confident commander tackling change, Mr. Allen now looks to some critics like an uncaring and unaccountable chief whose numerous restructurings wiped out $15 billion in earnings during the past decade. The breakup plan, initially hailed by Wall Street, is shaping up as a tacit admission that Mr. Allen's original vision—a "vertically integrated" empire of computers and communications—was a costly failure.[10]

Downsizing and Acting with Integrity

Reductions in workforce often suggest inconsistencies on the part of an organization and its leadership. To many, downsizing feels like a broken promise. Even if this is implicit, many believe that mutual loyalty means that layoffs occur only in the most extreme situations. In the worst cases, promises not to reduce staff have actually been made at some point in time. Then, due to leadership mistakes or changes in the marketplace, these promises are violated. On the other hand, an organization may act during the downsizing in a way that is inconsistent with its stated values. For example, many organizations today have values that emphasize the importance of people. While few firms guarantee employment, most maintain that their people are their "greatest asset" and deserving of "respect and support." Such values are questioned when a firm fires thousands of employees.

Similarly, downsizing can suggest a lack of integrity when it results in enormous savings to the company—yet the employees don't see any of these benefits. In many instances, downsizings have occurred simultaneously with rapid increases in the compensation of senior corporate leaders and of CEOs in particular. For example, a number of CEOs have recently received a great deal of criticism for multimillion-dollar compensations at the same time that their firms are reducing payrolls by the tens of thousands.[11]

Amid the pain of downsizing, increases in salary for the general employee population have lagged far behind increases at the executive level. The result is a perception of greed among those in leadership positions and an attitude of distrust toward them. In short, many employees believe they are paying the price to ensure that their corporations and leaders prosper.

Why are reductions skewed to affect one group or level within the organization when there is talk about acting as "one firm"? Why are some people, or groups, richly rewarded when the organization is stressing cost reduction? Why do politics seem to be more important than ability when the organization talks about pay for performance? Employees are bound to ask similar questions when their organization's integrity wavers in downsizing situations.

Downsizing and Demonstrating Concern

Some would argue that true concern means that layoffs would never occur. Others might say that firms that talk about concern for their employees while firing people are completely hypocritical. Most people, however, recognize that layoffs are sometimes required in order to compete in a fast-paced world. Consider the recent efforts by Chase to manage its merger with Chemical Bank effectively. This merger, like many in the financial services industry, has been driven by competitive pressures. Banks must dramatically alter the way they function and reduce their cost structure in order to survive. New nonbanking entities, such as brokerage firms, are offering customers lower fees along with new services. Those banks unable to improve their productivity significantly and generate new revenue through innovative products and services will ultimately fail. The Chase-Chemical merger is an attempt to create competitive advantage in anticipation of future challenges. The success of the new Chase will depend on how successfully it merges two very different organizations. The firm has used a variety of mechanisms to create a new culture and keep employees informed of changes. For example, it sends out *Merger Update,* a newsletter about progress. Senior leadership meets with employees in town-hall gatherings and training workshops. There is a twenty-four–hour 800 line for merger questions. There are senior management voice-mail messages before major announcements. In many respects, Chase's efforts set an example of how to manage a merger effectively.

One result of the merger, however, has been the elimination of thousands of jobs, and many remaining employees have become distrustful of all efforts to provide support. One disenchanted Chase employee noted that as a result of the merger, "You feel like you want to work in Japan or Sweden. A place where they take care of their people and their crippled. It's like a lost era here. It's like growing up. There's no more Santa Claus."[12] Other employees at Chase have begun circulating their own "underground" merger updates to express their feelings about the changes. One newsletter, under the banner of "frequently asked questions," included the following:

Why am I facing layoffs, why is my career in ruins, why can't I sleep at night?

Your largely insignificant life is being sacrificed to bring into existence the best banking and financial services company in the world, bar none, without par, without equal, post no bills, void where prohibited.

When will I know if I'm being laid off?

You, you, you, is that all you care about, you? Please understand that we need to think about "us," which probably doesn't include you. It's about time you started to think about the greater whole, buddy. . . . It should be an honor to be laid off.

Advice on how to ensure a job at the new Chase:

Take your boss to lunch. Buy him/her a gift (under the $250 limit, please). Tell him/her over and over again that your only hope, dream and aspiration is to serve for little or no pay and work inhuman hours to make this place the best banking and financial services company in the world, bar none, without par, without equal, post no bills, void where prohibited.[13]

The newsletter gives voice to employees' feelings of frustration and doom. The humor helps—but not enough.

Maintaining Trust amid Downsizing

A full description of how to deal effectively with the dilemmas of downsizing is beyond the scope of this book.[14] However, several actions are important in mitigating the impact on trust of reductions in the workforce. These actions include focusing on customers and markets, acting boldly, communicating directly and truthfully, and providing ample support.

Focusing on Customers and Markets

Keeping the people who remain with the firm focused on the needs of the business and its customers is extremely helpful in any downsizing. This approach begins with an explanation of the business reasons for the downsizing and the competitive challenges facing the firm. It extends into sustaining throughout the downsizing period a focus on key business challenges and the need to meet customer demands. The human costs of the reductions should not be ignored, however. Still, the larger objective must be kept in mind as the overall context for making the changes.

Consider, for example, the steps taken by Chaparral Steel to ensuring a market-driven approach. All of its nine hundred employees are considered members of its sales force and work directly with customers taking complaints. The firm also requires every employee to spend time each year visiting with customers and other companies to develop new ideas about how their firm can improve.[15] The goal is to provide all employees with direct knowledge of the competitive pressures facing the firm.

Acting Boldly

In some cases, leaders want to minimize the immediate impact of downsizings. They may therefore take less extreme action than is really required by the competitive situation. As a result, they end up having to go back for more reductions. Having one downsizing effort follow on the heels of another is particularly demoralizing. Some firms have been through five or more downsizing efforts over a ten-year period. Repeated downsizings risk the further alienation of those who have already been through one or more rounds of the process. For example, Unisys, the computer firm, has come under pressure for having undergone five restructurings in seven years. The result is a workforce that fears additional cuts and wonders if leadership has the answer to the problems facing their firm. While its case is extreme, firms must now change far more often than ever before. Therefore, it is better to act boldly initially and strive to reduce the number of downsizing initiatives that occur over time.

Communicating Directly and Truthfully

In downsizing situations, it is impossible to have too much information. Given the impact that downsizing has on everyone in the firm (both those who remain and those who leave), information is paramount. In particular, I have found that the accessibility of leadership—and of the senior leader in particular—can minimize some of the doubt and resentment that surface in these situations. Often, however, the senior person would rather not deal with the stressful aspects of a downsizing, so he or she delegates this responsibility to the human resources department or to an outplacement firm. But this approach often has negative results.

Some firms require years to recover from the mistakes made in the process of downsizing. In particular, a lack of honesty on the organization's part with regard to the need for downsizing and the process by which it will be managed can result in deep-seated suspicion. Surveys typically find that the majority of employees don't believe what management says, nor do they feel well informed of company plans.[16] In the worst cases, leadership has denied that a downsizing was forthcoming and then, when it did occur, misled people about the process. In some cases, there was little support for those affected as the leadership tried quickly to move beyond what was an uncomfortable and often embarrassing situation.

Contrast this with the approach followed by those who tell employees what they know as soon as possible and are willing to reveal when they don't have an answer to a particularly difficult issue. For example, one division within a large corporation made a decision to close a plant. On learning the news, the plant manager came into the facility and told people that the plant would close in six months and that he would do everything possible to ensure that the transition would be managed in a way that met their needs. He told them the facts as he knew them; he even shared those areas where he had no information. He told them when he would get back to them with more information and how they could ask questions of him and others. While the employees were not satisfied with the decision to close the plant, they still respect him for being honest with them and being supportive to the best of his ability.[17]

Providing Ample Support

Naturally, employees would prefer to keep their jobs. But the approach taken by a firm during a downsizing can have a significant impact on the level of trust people feel toward leadership and the organization as a whole. In many cases of reductions, a firm is in financial difficulty; thus, spending additional time and money on those who will be eliminated from the payroll may seem an unnecessary expense. But in the interests of the firm's credibility and the level of trust within the remaining workforce, the time and money are well spent.

GE was one of the first firms to reduce its workforce significantly as a means of strengthening its competitive position. During the restructuring of the 1980s, Welch made a great effort to provide support for those affected. GE provided employees with a number of options, including relocation, early retirement with full benefits, generous severance pay, retraining opportunities with preferential hiring, and outplacement services. The firm was also one of the first to provide long lead times in telling employees of layoffs (as much as one year in some cases). All of this was done before any commonly accepted approach to dealing with the human costs of restructuring had been established. This is not to minimize the impact of lost jobs on employees, their families, and the larger communities in which they live. But it is to say that GE sought to make a difficult, painful process less difficult and less painful.

A firm's policy on redeploying those whose positions are eliminated is important. In particular, every effort should be made to retain those who wish to remain with the firm (assuming that they have either the talent or potential to contribute to the downsized organization). This can be accomplished through reassignment and retraining. Transfers to new locales can also be used.

HP is a stellar example of a company that tries to keep people on board by finding them other jobs within the firm; as a result, it has sustained the faith of its employees even in the few cases where reductions have been necessary. More creative alternatives are also possible. When layoffs are impossible to avoid, a firm can also help employees find jobs outside the company.

Reengineering and Restructuring

Concurrent with the downsizing of corporate America over the past decade, we have seen massive restructuring efforts in most firms. These initiatives, in most cases, significantly change the structure of an organization as well as the roles and responsibilities of individuals. In some cases, these efforts focus on the macro level and involve reconfiguring the entire organization and the offerings it provides. In other cases, the changes are more detailed and result in new approaches to core work processes. In both cases, the long-term stability that characterized most corporations prior to the 1980s is undermined. Distrust is the result.

A vivid example of the potential for distrust in the wake of restructuring can be found at Quaker State. Historically the number one player in the motor-oil industry, the firm had fallen on hard times by the mid 1980s. Castrol and Pennzoil were offering distributors and customers aggressive marketing initiatives. Quaker was losing almost two points of market share a year before its board tried to stem the decline by bringing in a new CEO. They selected Herb Baum, a marketing expert from Campbell Soup, who knew almost nothing about the oil industry. Quaker's board was convinced that a fresh approach to marketing oil was essential in a stagnant industry.

Baum moved quickly. He started cutting costs and launching aggressive discounts and rebates to jump-start stagnant brands. He changed the name of Quaker's drive-through chain and created more appealing packaging. In focusing on marketing oil as one would any consumer product, Baum revised Quaker's advertising plan. He also refocused the business on lubricants and sold the firm's insurance business while making two major acquisitions. The turnaround included a management shake-up, replacing five of the six members of his management team. The results, to date, have been promising. Quaker is gaining share, and its stock has increased significantly since Baum took over.[18]

Baum then announced his next move in the effort to overhaul Quaker. He has decided that the company will leave its home of Oil City, Pennsylvania, for Dallas, Texas. Baum believes the city's remote location makes recruiting top talent difficult. Moreover, he asked only half of the corporate staff of three hundred to move to Dallas. Many feel Baum has betrayed them and the community that had a close relationship with Quaker for most of this century. Baum is convinced that a move to a more metropolitan location, near other related businesses, is vital for the continued growth of his firm. Most observers believe that Baum will have a significant challenge in rebuilding morale after the move.

This case illustrates a common theme in corporations today. CEOs are forcing significant changes that result in widespread layoffs and, in some cases, the relocation of entire organizations. The dilemma opposes competence, which in many cases requires bold actions, and concern for those affected by these moves. Trust, in a corporate setting, requires both results and concern. The balance between these competing forces is often elusive. To reach that balance, organizations need to focus on customer needs and use high-involvement approaches.

Focusing on Meeting Customer Needs

The anxiety that is aroused when organizations are undergoing significant changes can be mitigated, in part, by an ongoing focus on what remains the same—and this means, in particular, the customer. In as many ways as possible, organizations need to keep the customers' voice audible during the reengineering process. This can be done in a variety of ways, including involving customers on design and steering committees. The intent is twofold. First, this helps make sure the design is responsive to evolving customer needs. Second, this attempts to keep employees focused on the external, competitive need for change (versus the internal politics that can quickly dominate such efforts).

Most reengineering efforts that I have observed begin with either overly vague or widely extravagant performance targets. One of the advantages offered by reengineering, of course, is the possibility of moving beyond incremental change and making significant increases in performance. Yet employees need to understand the relationship between the change and customer needs. They also need to believe in the targets that are being set. Otherwise, they become cynical and will passively resist the change effort.

Using High-Involvement Approaches

One of the ironies of reengineering is that the process used to redesign the organization (top-down centralized control) is often at odds with the desired result (local accountability and authority). While reengineering an organization is not a democratic process, the key stakeholders inside the organization should be actively involved in the design process. Each organization will have a different set of stakeholders, but the list typically involves the senior leadership team, key functional leaders, team leaders in crucial areas, employees who are closest to the customers and the work itself, and people at all levels with the ability to influence others. Involving these groups is vital to any reengineering effort. The goal is real ownership for the changes and the process by which the organization moves forward.

As with many of the dilemmas outlined in this chapter, regular conversation about the obstacles and enablers to change is crucial.

The challenge is to get senior leadership (not the transition leaders or external consultants) to be highly visible during the change process. In particular, they should be willing to deal publicly with the tough issues that will inevitably surface as the change effort moves forward. They need to be passionate about the need for change and clear about the purpose of the change effort. They also need to be flexible in modifying the organization's approach as the process moves forward (without compromising the principles of the effort).

∽

Balancing the Dilemmas

Trust dilemmas are common in most large organizations. Business pressures pull firms in directions that inevitably create conflicts; if not properly managed, these conflicts create distrust. The pressure for short-term results, for example, threatens the foundation of trust as organizations downsize and restructure. The dilemmas discussed in this chapter show how the conflicts among these imperatives can become pronounced. These dilemmas and possible ways to ameliorate them are summarized here.

Issue	Action Steps
Strategic Mistakes	• Take responsibility for the problem • Extract learning from failures • Enforce accountability across all levels • Demonstrate immediate progress
Ethical Violations	• Take immediate action • Conduct an organizational audit • Establish appropriate controls

Brute Force Management	• Act on values and operating principles • Develop a culture where people matter • Stress development and growth
Downsizing	• Focus on customers and markets • Act boldly • Communicate directly and truthfully • Provide ample support
Reengineering and Restructuring	• Focus on meeting customer needs • Use high-involvement approaches

Even amid the tension that most firms face with regard to results, integrity, and concern, success is possible, as the examples illustrate. Hewlett-Packard, as much as any firm I know, has effectively managed these tensions. Naturally, it has on occasion slipped on one or more of the trust imperatives, yet it does serve as a useful benchmark of what a high-trust organization looks like in action. It demonstrates that by balancing the need for results, integrity, and concern, a company can successfully transform itself and thrive in today's highly turbulent and competitive times.

Further guidance for firms seeking to regain trust and for firms in which levels of trust are unacceptably low is found in Chapter Ten.

Chapter Ten

Regaining Lost Trust

Within most organizations and teams, an overall sense of trust—or distrust—evolves and becomes part of the informal culture. In cultures of trust, the comfort that people feel with each other appears natural and is usually implicit. High-trust organizations have the "collaborative capital" needed to sustain them through periods of turmoil. By comparison, in low-trust organizations, even those people who are inclined to trust others will gradually become more suspicious. In low-trust organizations, suspicion is always present even if it is an "undiscussable" subject. Low-trust organizations become stuck in destructive patterns that foster suspicion even during periods of improvement and progress.

The concept of a trust threshold (discussed in Chapter Two) helps explain the tenacity of distrust. In short, once someone's trust threshold has been crossed, trust quickly becomes distrust. And once lost, trust is not easily regained. In cultures of distrust, people take note of any behavior or event that confirms their suspicions. Their suspicions thus become self-perpetuating and highly resistant to change. In such cultures, people are also likely to ignore or discount any information that indicates that it is safe to let go of their distrust.

The Consequences of Distrust

We have only to look at AT&T for a prime example of what happens when suspicion feeds on itself. AT&T recently took out full-page advertisements in papers across the country soliciting job offers for the thousands of employees whose jobs would be eliminated in the firm's restructuring. This action, however, was viewed with considerable cynicism within the firm and by the press. Many believed that

AT&T was simply seeking to enhance its public image rather than truly working to help those who would be displaced. AT&T's actions were seen as corporate "spin control," motivated by a need to protect the corporation's image. Why this interpretation? AT&T had broken the trust of employees by significantly reducing the workforce over the course of a year. Those who lost their jobs and many who remained lost their faith in the firm; AT&T's actions had crossed their trust threshold. As a result, they interpreted AT&T's real actions to help those affected as self-serving and deceptive.

A similar scenario illustrating the power of distrust was played out, with larger effect, at Eastern Airlines in the late 1980s. Several years before its final shutdown, a milestone agreement had been drafted in which union members accepted deep cuts in wages, totaling $800 million, in return for stock in the company and representation on Eastern's board of directors. The agreement seemed to mark the beginning of a new era in management and labor relations in which understanding and cooperation would replace the adversarial relations of the past. Some believed the agreement would set a new standard for management and labor relations across America. Eastern, however, continued to face growing competition and smaller profit margins as a result of industry deregulation. Eastern's structure changed when union members became board members and shareholders, but relationships among the firm's key players held steady: the new era in management and labor relations never arrived. The gulf between management and labor that had grown deep and bitter over many years of adversarial relations remained.

As Eastern's CEO in the late 1980s, Frank Borman faced a deteriorating financial situation that made it impossible to repay the firm's outstanding debt. Creditors would defer Eastern's obligations only if Borman obtained new cost-cutting labor agreements. He went to his workforce and demanded a 20 percent cut in pay and changes in work rules that would increase productivity. Borman made it quite clear that if the workforce refused to accept these changes, the options were to sell the firm or file for Chapter 11. The company's pilots and attendants accepted his demands, believing the changes were the only way to save the company. But Eastern's machinists, having made major concessions in the past, refused to cooperate.

The machinists believed management was exaggerating the severity of the firm's financial situation and in some cases lying in order to win further concessions. Charles Bryan, head of the union, told his members that further givebacks would be demanded even if they accepted the current list of demands. Bryan would agree to further cuts only if a new chief executive officer was appointed. He stated that he would rather sell the airline than continue with Borman in charge. The union explored a wide range of options, including the possibility of bankruptcy, takeover by a rival firm, employee ownership, and a strike to prevent management from acting without labor's consent. According to one board member, as the range of options narrowed, Bryan decided that the devil he didn't know was better than the devil he knew. It was said that he preferred Frank Lorenzo, the head of a rival airline with a strident antiunion reputation, over Borman as Eastern's CEO because at least Lorenzo was a businessman with whom he could negotiate.[1]

And Bryan was not alone: a growing number of employees, knowledgeable about the airline industry and their company's internal affairs, had lost faith in Borman's leadership abilities. The firm had performed poorly under his stewardship and showed no signs of improving in the near future. Many believed they were suffering because of Borman's mismanagement. Employees were particularly disturbed because Eastern's $2.5 billion debt, the impetus for the most recent round of concession demands, had been incurred mainly as a result of Borman's purchase of new, and some thought unnecessary, aircraft.

Eastern's board concluded in a final late-night meeting that the current situation was untenable. The board did not force Borman to resign. Nor did it accept the 15 percent reduction Bryan was willing to offer by way of concessions. Instead, the airline was sold to Frank Lorenzo of Texas Air for $600 million. A weary senior Eastern management official approached Bryan near the end of the final negotiations to save the airline and said, "Charlie, I'm trying to control my temper. But right now, you just destroyed forty thousand jobs. I want them all to know that you're the guy that destroyed their jobs." Pointing to the room where the company's board was meeting, Bryan angrily replied, "There are the sixteen guys who did it." The headline in the *New York Times* after the sale read, "Failure at Eastern: Lack of Trust Seen."[2]

Within months, Borman and his staff were replaced by a management team from Texas Air. Lorenzo demanded that the union accept pay cuts of 60 percent in some job classifications. He also wanted to eliminate almost all work rules, seniority rights, and restrictions on outside contracting. The other unions at Eastern, angry with Bryan for refusing to accept Borman's demands a year earlier, were unwilling to honor a picket line if a strike was called. Bryan described his showdown with Lorenzo as "the kind of fight only one man walks away from." The dispute was marked by severe disruption of service, sale of the carrier's assets, numerous lawsuits, safety investigations initiated by the unions, several failed efforts to sell the airline—and eventual bankruptcy.

Several factors influenced the fall of Eastern, with the most significant being a harsher competitive environment and key strategic mistakes by senior leadership. Underlying those problems, however, lay a lack of trust, which undermined the firm's ability to adapt to a shifting business environment and to rebound from its mistakes. The various stakeholders at Eastern had become unwilling, or unable, to work toward a common goal. As a result, their firm ceased to exist.

As the conflict at Eastern so clearly illustrates, distrust, if allowed to go unchecked, can threaten an organization's ability to work through conflicts and build for the future. Without trust, the "collaborative capital" needed to conduct business is missing. Just as firms cannot function without sufficient financial capital, they cannot function without a reservoir of trust that enables them to deal constructively with conflict and crisis.

In organizations and teams with chronic levels of distrust, letting down one's guard by letting go of suspicion in what has been a hostile environment is perceived as being simply too risky. As a result, those seeking to overcome distrust face a daunting task. They are forced to take action far beyond what would be necessary in healthier situations. Common approaches to enhancing trust are simply insufficient; bold actions are required.

Assessing Distrust

A number of steps are useful in addressing distrust in an organization. One should first assess its pervasiveness throughout the organization, its impact, and its cause; only then can one go about devising solutions.

How Pervasive Is the Distrust?

Those seeking to overcome distrust should know whether levels of trust vary across the organization. Distrust may be found primarily within certain groups or at certain levels. This is not to say that the groups or levels in which distrust is highest are the source of the problem (instead, distrust is almost always a dynamic that involves all parts of an organization or team). But it does suggest that any action plan needs to take into account how people in different roles and different groups view the organization and its problems.

In determining the depth of trust and the scope of distrust in an organization, leaders need to ask the following questions:

- What is the level of trust within the organization?
- Does the level of trust vary across groups?
- Has the level of trust changed over time?
- What key events have created suspicion?

With each question, the leader seeks to determine the depth and breadth of distrust in the company. Answers to these questions may also help determine the impact of distrust.

What Is the Impact of the Distrust?

At Eastern, pervasive distrust was crippling. But not all distrust is damaging or even unhealthy; it may be natural and even useful. For example, some organizational members may begin to distrust an internal support group that has failed to deliver quality services. To continue to trust such a group would be foolhardy. Moreover, the impact of distrust toward this group is relatively minor with respect to the business at large. Or there may be competition among development groups to launch a new product. Some distrust is natural among these groups and should be expected.

In other cases, however, distrust may have reached the point where it is severely hurting the organization. The relationship between management and labor at Eastern fits this description. Other, more commonly found examples involve high levels of suspicion between groups (such as sales and manufacturing) that must collaborate if the firm is to be successful.

As a first step in determining the impact of distrust in an organization, ask the following questions:

- What are the overall consequences of low trust within the organization? With certain groups?
- Is distrust resulting in limited employee empowerment, which in turn inhibits our ability to meet customer needs?
- What impact is low trust having on our ability to work together as individuals and teams in meeting business objectives?
- Is distrust resulting in an inability to implement new initiatives effectively?

Next, having answered these questions, you need to move on to the cause or causes of the distrust.

What Has Caused the Distrust?

Those seeking to build trust first need to understand the primary causes of suspicion within an organization or team. Often, people will attribute distrust to personality conflicts among key individuals. This might be the case: leadership might—intentionally or not—contribute to the culture of suspicion rather than one of cooperation.

More typically, however, a larger set of forces is at work to sustain distrust. There might be an organizational structure that creates unhealthy competition among individuals and groups. Or the reward system either fails to acknowledge people fairly or creates a situation in which people compete for limited resources. Or perhaps organizational policies and practices force individuals in different groups to distrust one another. For example, budgeting systems in which groups compete for limited resources encourage groups and individuals to inflate their needs in order to secure more funds. This effectively rewards people for being less than honest and sets the stage for distrust.

The goal in the assessment, then, is to move beyond superficial explanations and determine the "deep" cause of suspicion within groups. The following questions can be a help:

- Which formal structures, practices, or policies contribute to distrust?
- Are there any informal organizational norms or values that create suspicion?
- Is the distrust within the organization primarily a failure to achieve results? If so, is this due primarily to individuals, key groups, or the firm at large?
- Is the distrust within the organization primarily a failure to act with integrity? Does the organization have a history of acting in ways that lack integrity? Do any of the key players have this history?
- Is the distrust within the organization primarily a failure to demonstrate concern? Has the organization failed to demonstrate concern for its members? Have the leaders?

Can Distrust Be Counterbalanced?

To begin to counterbalance the distrust and nurture trust, leaders must first determine if the distrust observed within the organization is linked to a failure of results, integrity, or concern. These trust imperatives, examined in detail in the earlier chapters of this book, provide clues to the root causes of suspicion. Leaders will need to gather information about what current practices or policies relative to each area are contributing to the distrust. Typically, pervasive distrust will involve all three imperatives, but one may be paramount.

Once the cause has been determined, those conducting the assessment are wise to solicit ideas from employees about how to create an environment where people can collaborate to achieve business results. To this end, the questions might include:

- What needs to change so that leadership no longer contributes to the culture of suspicion within the organization?
- What should leadership do to contribute to and support trust within the organization?

- How can the formal structures, practices, or policies that currently contribute to distrust be changed?
- How can the informal organizational norms or values that create suspicion be changed?
- How would a high-trust organization operate? What would be different from how the firm operates today?

The purpose in asking these questions, along with those in earlier sections, is to gather enough data to inform key actions. First it is important to understand, however, that in many organizations, an assessment is more effective if conducted in a low-key manner without a great deal of fanfare. Taking a highly visible approach in a low-trust situation can exacerbate already existing tensions.

On the other hand, we could argue that trust begins with openness around key issues. If the assessment is conducted in a more visible way, then it is a good idea to link the process to the achievement of specific business objectives. In other words, those conducting the assessment are seeking to determine what is getting in the way of the collaboration needed to achieve business results. Trust is seen as a means to an end—not an end in itself.

Overcoming Distrust

Overcoming high levels of distrust requires a break from past organizational practices. A disruption of "business as usual" signals that the organization is committed to moving forward. Specifically, the organization needs to make it clear that the old way of operating is being replaced by a more collaborative approach. This break from the past may involve changes in leadership or in the structure of the organization. It could also, however, involve more informal changes, such as leadership being direct and honest for the first time in years about the problems facing the firm. While a complete break from the past is impossible and in most cases undesirable, bold actions are needed to restore trust.

Given the robust nature of distrust, isolated efforts will not work; instead, organizations are wise to implement an integrated set of changes. The range of options includes changes to the organization's leadership, architecture, and culture. The various initiatives suggested here should be integrated into a coherent approach in order to build on each other for the best chance of success.

Changing the Leadership

In extreme situations, the fastest and in some cases only way to move beyond distrust is to change those in key leadership positions. Not every senior leader needs to be replaced; however, those most closely associated with the past events that gave rise to distrust may be unable to shed the negative perceptions that people in the organization have about them. And perception, in the realm of trust, counts for a great deal. Further, individuals with a long history of antagonistic relationships are often unable to switch to a more collaborative arrangement.

Those with the authority to make changes (in many cases, this involves the board) must assess to what degree the existing leadership can move beyond the past. They need to determine the critical mass of people to be replaced if the company is to take a new approach. In some cases, this may involve the movement of a few key individuals. In other cases, the majority of the leadership team needs to be replaced, along with those in key functional or group assignments.

Those coming into new positions of leadership, as well as those who have stayed on, can use the first few months after the change to demonstrate new ways of thinking and acting. The specific themes that are best emphasized will vary depending on the factors that have given rise to distrust. For example, say that the old leadership acted in ways that lacked integrity. The new leaders should illustrate the importance of integrity in their own behavior and the actions of the organization. The same may hold for the other trust imperatives (achieving results and demonstrating concern). Of course, this change in leadership must involve more than pronouncements: in low-trust situations, people discount words and believe only what they see.

Rallying Around a Crisis or Opportunity

Low-trust situations call for an external force to pull people together. This can be a crisis (the firm is nearing bankruptcy) or an opportunity (the firm can double in size if a hot new product can be brought to market in half the usual time). A crisis can force those who have historically been at odds to behave in different ways. Some organizations refer to this as the "burning platform" that forces people to take a leap of faith toward working in new ways, since the old way is obviously doomed.

But other conditions must be present for an external crisis to have a productive effect, as the demise of Eastern illustrates. Without the right people at the top, a crisis will only exacerbate the distrust that already exists. The key is to identify a force great enough to pull people together and then work under stress to achieve an outcome that all value. In general, the new leaders must create a common vision and a shared set of goals. The use of a crisis—or an opportunity—should be related to this larger vision for the entire organization.

Breaking the Structural Frame

Low-trust organizations are almost always characterized by rigid boundaries among organizational groups. These boundaries may be based on hierarchy (different levels distrust each other), function (different functional groups distrust each other), or business unit (different geographical or customer units distrust each other). New structural linkages are needed to overcome a history of isolation or conflict. This type of structural change may involve a reconfiguration of the primary groups within an organization (taking, for example, functional groups and creating customer-focused groups). Or the structural changes may decouple organizations that have been forced into unnatural alliances, creating tension and yielding little in return.

In less extreme cases, the changes needed may not impact the primary groupings within an organization. Instead, the firm may develop new ways of coordinating activities across groups. Examples of linkages include steering committees, liaison roles, aligned group and individual objectives, common management processes, cross-group meetings or forums, and multigroup task or project teams. The goal is to develop a variety of formal approaches that will ensure closer collaboration.[3] Matrix structures, where dual reporting relationships are created, should be used cautiously as a coordinating mechanism. These structures usually require a great deal of skill and effort—competencies that may not be available in a low-trust organization—to work effectively.

Eliminating Trust-Eroding Practices

Moving beyond a culture of distrust requires diligence in changing old patterns of behavior. Many people in low-trust environments will continue to work in ways that fuel suspicion unless they are shown the need to behave differently. For example, a functional leader may refuse to collaborate with colleagues on key business initiatives, or a senior leader may refuse to push accountability into the organization (and instead keep it for himself or herself). The specifics will vary depending on a firm's culture. The response to those exhibiting "old behavior," however, should be consistent and, when needed, tough. A new way of operating cannot last if key individuals are allowed to function in ways that reinforce distrust and suspicion.

In addition, low-trust situations are often plagued by management systems that sustain distrust. These systems become lightning rods for suspicion. For example, some systems result in groups and individuals lowering their performance objectives in order to increase their likelihood of making their targets. If this is allowed, the organization ends up rewarding those who are less aggressive and, in some cases, less honest.

One of the most important policies to examine in relation to trust is the organization's reward system. The goal, in general, is to create reward systems that encourage individual achievement along with shared ownership for organizational performance. Systems must be crafted carefully to avoid simply creating new zero-sum situations (where individuals and groups believe they must outperform others in order to be successful). For example, many organizations have traditionally forced a bell-shaped distribution of performance ratings. This system ensures that superior performance across the board will not be rewarded (since some employees must fall on the lower end of the performance continuum). This forces employees to compete against each other for recognition and rewards. To prevent this effect, the leadership needs to establish collective rewards that reinforce collaboration and identification with the entire firm. The nature of these reward systems will vary but typically will include profit sharing and group bonuses.

Motorola has taken a different tactic with its annual worldwide employee competition on quality and customer satisfaction. A set of well-known criteria (including involvement of all team members in the project) is used to evaluate the results of teams across the firm. The projects are screened, and at year's end, twelve finalists are recognized in a company-wide event. Their accomplishments are publicized through employee newsletters that include photographs of the winners. The entire process, while resulting in a few winners, is designed to make all who enter feel like they have made a contribution and are making progress.[4]

The leadership task within low-trust organizations and teams is to scrap practices that provoke distrust and replace them, as necessary, with more collaborative processes. For example, some firms have systems that reward individuals for their suggestions. If not properly managed, a suggestion system can result in secrecy among employees. People keep their ideas to themselves in order to win financial awards, thus restricting the flow of information among individuals and groups. A restrictive suggestion system can be replaced with approaches that emphasize organizational learning and collective achievement of results.

Organizations can be well served by simply eliminating some systems and not putting others in their place. Consider, for example, one successful retailer's approach to an employee handbook. In most firms, the handbook, containing all types of policies and restrictions, fills several large binders. At Nordstrom, it is significantly smaller: half a page, to be exact. It reads,

> Welcome to Nordstrom. We're glad to have you with our company. Our number one goal is to provide outstanding customer service. Set both your personal and professional goals high. We have great confidence in your ability to achieve them.
>
> Nordstrom rules: Use your good judgment in all situations. Please feel free to ask your department manager, store manager or division general manager any question at any time.[5]

Stressing Teamwork in Order to Achieve Results

Most organizations have some values or operating principles that underscore the importance of collaboration and teamwork. However, these values are often perceived as "all talk," which only produces more cynicism. People wonder why they should be expected to support the idea of teamwork when they see their leaders acting in self-serving ways. With new leadership, the organization has an opportunity to make a strong statement about the need for collaboration across levels and groups. The emphasis on teamwork should ideally be related to specific business challenges and needs and linked to clear performance targets. In other words, teamwork is a means to achieve specific business objectives (rather than something that it would be "nice to do" if people are so inclined). In particular, as described in Chapter Six, the senior team of an organization should strive to move past the rivalries that are evident in most firms.

In many firms, for example, functional and geographic groups operate in a largely autonomous manner. In more extreme cases, these groups are in conflict and spend more time fighting with each other than working together to meet targets or surpass the competition. The senior team can set an example of collaboration and mutual support. As a team, they may align around a common set of goals that cut across different groups. As individuals, they may work together on cross-group initiatives or provide active support for initiatives sponsored by those in another group. Through their words and actions, the leadership can reinforce the need for collaboration and support. True collaboration in the organization can happen only if the senior team can align on a common set of objectives and work together to make them happen.

Capitalizing on Collective Wins

New approaches to working together that reflect higher levels of trust will ultimately fail if they don't produce results. In other words, people will go a certain distance on faith, but eventually they want to see concrete benefits resulting from a different way of working together. Recovery from distrust requires some quick "wins" to reinforce the benefits of working collaboratively. To the degree possible, these wins should benefit most, if not all, of the organization. They can also specifically demonstrate the benefits of collaboration among groups that have historically been adversaries.

IBM provides a recent example of capitalizing on these types of wins to recover trust. After reducing its workforce by over 125,000 people over the past decade, the stability and loyalty of the past were gone. In assuming his role as CEO, Lou Gerstner stressed the importance of winning in the marketplace. He said that the problems facing the firm could not be solved unless the fundamentals were fixed and people worked together to win back customers and market share. After a year of solid performance gains, IBM gave its employees in 1996 an increase in pay and bonuses of 8 percent—far more than the national average of 4 percent.

It is equally important to communicate these wins across the organization in order to capitalize on them. The goal of such communication should not be merely public relations but a sincere desire to share news of the progress being made and of the lessons learned about collaboration. The style of communicating these lessons will vary from one firm to another; some firms may decide to publicize specific cases of successful collaboration within the organization as inspiration for others.

A Case of Recovery: Continental Airlines

As we have said, recovery from low levels of trust requires a clear understanding of the factors that have produced the suspicion. In the worst cases, the need for results, integrity, and concern have all been violated. Moving beyond distrust then requires a complete turnaround in these business fundamentals.

As mentioned earlier, one especially notable example of recovery from distrust is that of Continental Airlines. In the 1980s and early 1990s, Continental had a well-earned reputation as an inferior airline. It filed for bankruptcy twice. Some, including its own leadership, described the firm as a "tenth-place company," reflecting its rank among major carriers in the United States. It was dead last in customer satisfaction. In fact, in almost every key performance measure, the airline was last among the major carriers.

Employees were dispirited to the point that some removed symbols of their Continental affiliation when outside work. For example, some mechanics and pilots would take logos off their shirts and hats in order to avoid the negative comments they would hear once people knew they worked for Continental. Employees distrusted leadership; this was partly the negative legacy of Frank Lorenzo, whom most employees believed could not be trusted to keep his promises.

The turnaround involved a number of dramatic moves by Gordon Bethune, the newly appointed CEO. He began by bringing in Greg Brenneman as the firm's chief operating officer. The two had worked together before and shared a common managerial philosophy. Their goals were to restore accountability and pride in the dispirited firm. Brenneman, a former consultant with a wide base of experience, notes, "I have never seen a company in as much disarray. The fundamentals were broken beginning with a route and pricing approach that was just plain stupid. Moreover, there was a level of distrust beyond anything I have experienced. People distrusted management and refused to believe anything they said. Those in different functional groups would spend most of their time fighting with each other rather than responding to customer needs. It was in much worse shape than I assumed on making the decision to join Gordon."[6]

In short order, they made a number of dramatic moves designed to rebuild the airline. Even though trust was not their primary concern, we can look at their changes from the point of view of the trust imperatives of results, integrity, and concern. After all, trust, as we've said before, is best approached indirectly by concentrating on improving the fundamentals that build and sustain it.

Achieving Results

Bethune and Brenneman began with a series of bold moves to change the firm's financial performance. Their basic approach, called the "Go Forward" plan, stressed a few fundamentals. First, they discontinued many of Continental's unprofitable routes and closed the low-fare, no-frills division (dubbed Continental Light). Second, they revised Continental's pricing to increase revenue in markets that would support such increases. Third, they improved the quality of the Continental product by reintroducing meals on short flights, repainting planes, and remodeling key terminals. The impact of reducing cost and increasing revenue was evident immediately as the financial situation began to improve.

One of the primary forces behind many of the these changes was Ben Baldanza, who was brought in from United Parcel Service to revamp Continental's pricing and route scheduling. Changes at the top continued with the eventual replacement of fifty of the top sixty-one executives. Twenty new hires were brought in to build world-class talent in key areas of the business. The reward structure was completely revised to focus on the immediate improvement of fundamental business results. At the top, this meant a bonus plan with significant incentives for improvements early in the financial year (resulting in significant benefits if the business turned around quickly).

Rewards beyond the executive ranks were also revised to focus on a few key areas. In particular, Bethune and Brenneman wanted everyone in the organization to work to improve on-time performance and baggage handling (which were determined to be of primary importance to airline passengers). A bonus system was devised to reward every employee $65 each month if Continental placed second or third in on-time performance and baggage handling and $100 if it placed first. Again, the results were immediate; Continental began to show improvement and within a year placed at the top of the rankings.

Acting with Integrity

The new leadership team at Continental was the tenth in ten years. Employees were cynical about any new program and had no reason to believe that the new team would be any different from past leadership. Most employees simply didn't believe any promise made by leadership. Bethune and Brenneman began by following through on their commitments—consistently and visibly.

- They said teamwork at the top was critical and replaced those who could not or would not work as part of a team.
- They said employees were the key to the turnaround and, as one indication of this belief, remodeled the employee work areas in many of their terminals.
- They said employees were equipped to make sound business judgments and took the firm's nine-inch policy manual and burned it in a public display of the need for empowerment. They dismantled the security cameras that were used to monitor employees in the work areas.
- They said on-time performance and baggage handling were key and devised a reward system to back up their statements.

- They said that improving the organization's operations was essential and opened an 800 line staffed by pilots, flight attendants, and gate personnel to deal with issues within the firm. They made a commitment that staff would get back to people within forty-eight hours on any issue or opportunity for improvement.
- They said that unprofitable routes would be eliminated and did so despite the huge investment made by previous leadership.

These are just a few examples of how the leadership demonstrated its intent to turn a history of broken promises around and follow through on their commitments to employees.

The new team also started practicing a more open approach (in contrast to the previous leadership, which had often kept information from employees). "We strive to tell everyone everything we can," Brenneman says. "We want a culture with open dialogue and straight answers. In terms of our work with employees, we have been direct with them even when they don't like the answer. Our goal is not to please everyone but instead for them to trust what we tell them is the truth. You can't work the tough issues we face unless everyone, starting with the senior team, trusts one another."[7]

Demonstrating Concern

The new leadership team at Continental was intent on demonstrating their concern for the firm's employees. They gave generous severance packages to those removed from the top leadership cadre. They initiated a series of town-hall meetings that brought Bethune and Brenneman to each of Continental's facilities. Within months of taking charge, the two senior leaders of the firm had traveled to Continental's main terminals and met with thousands of employees. These were informal sessions in which the leaders laid out their strategies and answered employee questions and concerns. They returned phone calls from employees directly and, whenever possible, worked to get out of their offices on the twentieth floor of the headquarters building.

Since this effort began, Continental has gone from worst to first in every segment of the airline industry. The airline was recently ranked first in customer satisfaction among the nine major

U.S. carriers on long-distance flights (in contrast to a last-place finish the year before). Throughout 1996, Continental led the industry in on-time arrivals, baggage handling, and fewest complaints. These results reflect a dramatic turnaround in its financial performance, showing profitable results quarter after quarter (and making money for the first time since 1978). The stock has appreciated tenfold over a two-year period. Employee morale has also improved. All told, Continental has demonstrated remarkable recovery, proving that an organization can successfully overcome a legacy of distrust.

Moving from Distrust to Trust

In low-trust situations, incremental improvements cannot counterbalance the weight of suspicion that has built up over time. Overcoming such distrust requires courage, bold action, and tenacity. Courage is needed to initiate the actions that will move an organization or team beyond suspicion. Courage is needed to make tough calls concerning people and their ability to work together.

Bold action is required if people are to let go of their suspicions. These actions might involve total honesty about a firm's weaknesses and mistakes, changes at the top, the restructuring of its units, or the elimination of traditional management practices and policies. The actions needed to overcome distrust cannot consist of form rather than substance. Given the skepticism that exists in cultures of distrust, superficial actions will not work.

Overcoming distrust also requires tenacity. Those seeking to move their organizations beyond distrust cannot place their hopes on isolated, one-time change efforts. The various actions taken to overcome distrust should be part of an integrated change agenda that persists over time and deals with larger business issues. Such actions might include the following:

- *Change the leadership as needed* to ensure so that those in key roles can work in a more collaborative manner.
- *Rally around a crisis or opportunity* to galvanize people to work more collaboratively.
- *Break the structural frame* so that any historical boundaries contributing to the problems are removed.

- *Eliminate practices that erode trust* and replace them with practices and systems that reinforce collaboration and successful realization of key trust imperatives. Fire or otherwise redirect those who foster suspicion and act in self-serving ways at the expense of the organization's success.
- *Stress teamwork in order to achieve results.* Articulate, in a new and credible manner, the business need for collaboration across levels and groups.
- *Capitalize on collective wins.* Demonstrate that a more collaborative approach works and can provide concrete benefits to all.

A coordinated strategy to improve trust, linked to other organizational improvement initiatives, requires up-front planning and discipline in execution—considerably more discipline than one that is not coordinated. Still, even the best change plans will take years to be fully implemented because people are typically reluctant to let go of suspicion. Progress in overcoming distrust is slow and, in most cases, frustrating. Yet allowing the level of trust within an organization to erode is akin to allowing financial reserves to decline. The organization desperately needs the "collaborative capital" that trust affords, particularly during turbulent times, as we will see in the next chapter.

Chapter Eleven

Sustaining Trust into the Future

I recently spoke to a group of executives on the central importance of trust in successful businesses. One member of the audience asked why we should be concerned about trust if an organization is achieving its financial targets. He believed firms could reach their goals without trust. My response was to agree that organizations with low trust can achieve short-term results. As a consultant, I have seen firms in which people were extremely suspicious of one another, viewed others as threats, and valued power more than a collaborative work to meet a common set of goals. In such firms, internal political maneuvering consumes enormous amounts of time and energy. These are the firms in which only the strong and the manipulative advance. Yet some of these firms do achieve their short-term goals through "brute force" management. In my experience, however, each has suffered over the long term because their cultures have stifled the open debate of critical issues and the effective implementation of new competitive strategies. Chronic suspicion does eventually take its toll.

The cost of suspicion is also growing. Sustainable success in today's business world requires levels of trust far beyond what was needed even a decade ago. Simply put, a new set of market realities make trust more essential; now, when trust is effectively capitalized on, it offers a more significant competitive advantage than in years past. We are forced to deal with the dilemmas of trust because of new competitive pressures. Consider the following:

- Successful firms learn to master the complexities of constant change. Without trust, organizations lack the agility required to keep pace with rapidly changing markets. People in low-trust cultures will resist change at every turn.

• Successful firms give their people the freedom they need to perform in rapidly changing markets. Without trust, empowerment is no more than a corporate slogan with little real impact. Low-trust cultures are characterized by bureaucratic policies and procedures that limit individual creativity and initiative.

• Successful firms develop formal and informal means of ensuring collaborative working relationships both internally (among members of the firm) and externally (with outside suppliers and partners). Alignment around goals and coordinated action are impossible when trust is lacking.

Managing change, fostering empowerment, capitalizing on collaboration—each is critical in today's business world. Each requires a foundation of trust.

Cultures of trust are found in many firms. Some are smaller organizations where people are familiar with one another and function as an extended family. Other firms with high levels of trust are much larger: Hewlett-Packard, Motorola, Levi Strauss, 3M, and Toyota. Each of these corporations has developed a unique culture that balances the imperatives of achieving results, acting with integrity, and demonstrating concern. Each strives to capitalize on their high-trust cultures to the benefit of customers, employees, and shareholders.

Toyota, for example, is the benchmark firm in the automotive industry. Its performance in terms of quality and cost are world class. Many factors have contributed to Toyota's success; its culture of collaboration has been a key. Close working relationships among Toyota's employees and with its external suppliers have produced a system that is superior to any in its industry. Toyota has delivered "hard" results, in part through attention to "softer" cultural factors. In particular, Toyota has extended responsibility to the lowest possible levels in the organization and supported employees through a range of programs, including job security.

> The Toyota lean manufacturing system, which is a systematization of communally organized workplace, has led to enormous productivity improvements as well, indicating that community and efficiency can go together. . . . There is no necessary tradeoff, in other

words, between community and efficiency; those who pay attention to community may indeed become the most efficient of all.[1]

Inarguably, Toyota has created an industrial community that cares about its members and delivers superior results.

Hewlett-Packard is another visible example of a large organization with high levels of trust. The firm is primarily known for developing innovative information technology (such as printers which revolutionized the low-end of the market). It has thrived in a highly competitive industry that has humbled firms such as Apple and DEC. HP is also known for having one of the most positive organizational cultures of any firm in the world. In particular, it has a unique set of management philosophies and practices [2] that have resulted in a high-trust organization.

HP's employee survey results support the conclusion that it is a high-trust company. In the area of achieving results, for example, 84 percent of the firm's U.S. employees believe HP is well managed—35 percentage points higher than norms within its industry. In the area of acting with integrity, two-thirds of the firm's employees believe its management can be trusted to tell the truth (20 percentage points higher than industry norms) and act in a fair manner (19 percentage points higher). In the area of demonstrating concern, two-thirds of its employees believe HP's management is interested in the welfare of employees (15 percentage points higher than norms) and 75 percent believe employees are treated with respect regardless of their job (17 percentage points higher).[3] HP, in total, while being far from perfect, scores much higher than other firms on each of the three trust imperatives. It has pushed further than most firms in building the foundation of trust that is needed to compete in today's business environment.

HP has been able to transform itself, in part because of its unique culture. With the simple goal of creating a firm in which they personally would like to work, the founders built an organizational culture that serves as a model in balancing trust's various demands. The firm has grown dramatically and produced impressive financial results in a highly competitive industry. It has acted with integrity both in terms of its ethical values and its consistent adherence to a well-known set of principles. HP has also supported employee growth and well-being. It demonstrates that a high-trust culture is able to change faster and more effectively than its competitors. In the 1970s, for example, HP moved from being an instrument company to a computer company—a shift of a magnitude that few firms have successfully negotiated. HP is now undergoing another transformation as it moves beyond being a hardware producer to being a provider of multimedia products and services. In addition to these broad transformations, HP has continually altered its divisional structure in order to address marketplace conditions and competitive threats. Business units are created, closed, or merged depending on market factors. Again, few firms can manage the degree of change that HP has experienced. Trust has been a critical element in enabling HP to do so successfully.

Lessons Learned

We have seen numerous examples of the potential that trust offers in sustaining business success. In examining the successes of Toyota and Motorola, among others, we can extract a few summary lessons on the role of trust in organizational life.

Trust Is a Resource on a Par with Other Forms of Capital

Most firms keep an active watch on their financial resources. They understand that sufficient capital is needed in order to seize new opportunities as well as to deal with the adversity that strikes all firms at certain points in their history. Each significant decision is evaluated against the capital required. Few firms, however, give the same attention to the "collaborative capital" of their organization. Trust, as a form of capital, can be as important as a firm's financial resources. As with financial capital, trust must be protected and not allowed to drop to precarious levels. This is particularly important because trust, once lost, is extremely difficult to recover. Overcoming high levels of distrust and all the problems it creates can take years and a great deal of effort.

Viewing trust as a form of capital underscores that it is an asset that offers a competitive advantage (just as financial capital does).[4] But like money, trust is not a panacea. Trust is simply a resource on which to draw. It provides no assurance of business success. It is an enabler that allows other organizational structures, policies, and practices to work much more effectively. Only through good organizational design and the modeling work of senior teams can it be capitalized on to its full extent.

As a consultant in the area of organizational design, I quickly learned that elegant design is not enough. Designs that make a great deal of sense in terms of competitive realities often fail because of the distrust that exists within an organization or group. Distrust prevents alignment around and effective implementation of a design solution. Leaders in low-trust organizations must either try to implement an "ideal" that will most likely fail due to a lack of collaboration—or they must settle for an inferior design that they think they can implement given the culture they have created (or inherited). For example, many organizations that are providing global products and services must adopt some form of matrix structure (in which people have multiple reporting relationships). This often occurs when global product responsibility is shared with regional groups. Yet these structures, which make sense on paper, cannot work unless the leaders of the global product groups can work collaboratively with the leaders of the firm's regional groups. Trust, when present, enables this complex design to work. In its absence, a superior design will fail.

At the other extreme, I have seen organizations that are effective despite structural designs that would make the purist wince. They are far from elegant; typically, they have evolved over time and are plagued by redundancies and inconsistencies. From a logical perspective, these designs should fail. Yet they work because the people in the organization trust one another and compensate for the design's inherent weaknesses. I am working with one firm that split its product lines into groups with significant overlap. In some cases, the groups had similar product offerings and were targeting the same customers. The firm eventually cleaned up the design. But its "messy" design had worked for years because the principals in the firm were able to coordinate their activities and effectively deal with conflicts when they arose. Trust, in this case, made what was inferior better than could have been predicted on paper.

The role of trust as an enabler to organizational success is even more evident when examining senior teams. Many teams are far less effective than the sum of their parts. In other words, the members of the team, as individuals, have capabilities that outstrip the actual achievements of the team. In particular, there are situations where the talents of extremely gifted people are wasted because of the suspicion that exists among team members. This situation is the norm in most of the teams I have observed over my years of consulting. And it is becoming worse as more organizations turn to teams as the answer to their difficulties. We are populating organizations with teams that often lack the foundation of trust needed for success.

There are many cases, however, in which a team is capable of achievements far beyond what one would expect from the individuals on it. In these situations, team members respect each other's talent, work collaboratively toward a common goal, and take an active interest in each other's success.

One of the first things I look for in working with a senior group is the level of trust among its members. I have seen three main indicators of trust in senior groups: openness, respect, and alignment.

- *Openness.* One sign of trust is the willingness of members to be open with each other, particularly regarding problems. High-trust teams are able to bring difficult information and issues to the surface and work through them in an effective manner.
- *Respect.* Mutual respect for each other's ability and a willingness to build on the ideas of others is another sign of trust. In high-trust groups, people are less interested in proving their ability or getting their way and more interested in developing the best answer to a particular problem or opportunity.
- *Alignment.* A third indication of trust is alignment, which consists of coordination among team members as they implement team decisions. Members of high-trust teams agree to support each other once a decision has been made. They can debate the merits of different approaches but then move forward with one voice in implementing their decisions.

Trust Will Replace Loyalty as the Primary Bond Within Organizations

For decades, organizational life was constructed around an informal loyalty contract. The firm's end of the contract was to provide lifetime employment and career advancement based on seniority (as well as merit). In turn, employees would behave in a dutiful manner (including working at scheduled times, moving when transferred, following the organization's chain of command, and honoring company polices). This approach continued until competitive forces intervened. Specifically, the need to improve productivity forced a dramatic change in the loyalty contract. Firms, seeking to cut costs, radically reduced their workforces. Underperforming units were closed or sold. Outsourcing work to external suppliers became a common approach to reducing cost or enhancing performance. In turn, many employees shifted their loyalty from their firms to their profession or craft. They sought new career opportunities without a great deal of consideration for the impact their departure would have on their firms. They refused transfers away from their homes and demanded more say in how their work was performed. In sum, the loyalty contact that had been dominant at midcentury was now under siege.

A recent nationwide poll by the *New York Times* suggests the magnitude of this shift. A large majority of employees in the survey, over 70 percent, indicated that loyalty within their firms is declining while internal competition among coworkers is increasing.[5] These findings can be seen as an indictment of corporations seeking profit above all else. From this viewpoint, loyalty will return when corporations act more responsibly in seeking to avoid layoffs.

Another way of viewing the decline of loyalty, however, is to acknowledge that the global market will continue to force firms and nations to become more competitive. Striving for this competitive advantage will occur through a variety of approaches, including the redeployment of people. Already, cold economic realities are resulting in corporations using highly autonomous and flexible networks of individuals and teams. Firms have no choice but to embrace flatter, more flexible organizational structures in order to compete. The new competitive environment requires more independence and more collaboration. The result, in the language of consultants, is the "loosely coupled yet highly aligned" organization.

Trust is the foundation on which these firms and the teams within them will operate. Working toward the achievement of a common goal through empowerment and teamwork is impossible in an atmosphere of chronic distrust. Organizations are increasingly dependent on relationships with a wide range of people, and these relationships are more voluntary than mandatory. These types of relationships, such as joint ventures and business networks, require sufficient levels of trust among those involved. Without trust, these new networked organizations quickly revert to traditional hierarchical corporations or break apart altogether.[6]

Forms of loyalty that result in paternalistic practices, which detach people from bottom-line realities, cannot survive in a world in which productivity improvements are essential. The loyalty contract of the past stands in the way of building true competitive strength. The alternative, however, is not simply to treat each other as resources to be used when necessary. Treating each other as simple commodities denies the need for people to develop relationships based on mutual understanding and respect. And business success itself requires sufficient collaboration among a diverse group of people.

Trust is replacing loyalty as a way of bonding people into collective enterprises. Trust grows with effective collaboration in meeting the competitive challenges facing a firm. In contrast, loyalty, at its most extreme, is based on obligations independent of market realities. Several years ago, I worked with a firm that defined loyalty as guaranteed lifetime employment regardless of market forces or the performance of people within the firm. In other words, you were assured of a job and of pay increases as long you followed the direction set out by leadership. Loyalty, in this case, prevented the firm from tackling the tough issues it faced and, over time, made it less competitive. Trust is thus a more realistic and ultimately more beneficial way of building the human bonds needed in any organization.

Trust Is Important Internally and Externally

Trust is not simply an issue between organizations and their members; it is as important with customers, suppliers, and partners as it is with employees. Many of the dynamics discussed in this book—from the role of trust in business success to the imperatives that support it—can be applied to relations with external groups. Spend time talking with people at a high-trust firm such as Hewlett-Packard and you will most likely hear about relationships with customers. The firm believes customers use its products and services because they trust what the firm represents (innovative, high-value products and services). Its internal culture is closely linked to the ability to develop this type of reputation in the marketplace.

In the best firms, trust extends to relations with customers. Achieving results, acting with integrity, and demonstrating concern are the essentials for trust between a firm and its customers, just as they are for trust within the organization. One would be hard pressed to find a firm with low levels of trust among its employees that has built high levels of trust with its customers.

Similarly, the strong network of suppliers used by firms like Toyota are based on long-term relationships of trust. These relationships are a critical element in Toyota's ability to produce high-quality, low-cost vehicles. In other words, a long-standing and open partnership between a company and its suppliers can produce results superior to a simple market-based approach, where open bidding attempts to obtain the best price and quality. These supplier networks depend on complete honesty about ways of improving the product or service being provided and the best way to distribute the returns from such efforts. These types of relationships require a level of interdependence that goes far beyond the contractual relationship itself.

Trust Is Gained by Attention to the Fundamentals

Several years ago, I watched a CEO give a passionate speech on the topic of quality. He was committing to a new way of operating and holding himself, his team, and the organization accountable for results. At the end of the speech, I turned to a colleague and said, "Nothing will happen. He has just raised expectations with no intent of following through. I wish he had said nothing and let his actions convince people of his sincerity." Unfortunately, I was right. No real progress was made at the firm. People became more cynical. The CEO lost credibility.

Talk is cheap with regard to trust. We build trust by delivering results that are consistent with the expectations of those who depend on us. We build trust by fulfilling our promises and acting in a consistent and predictable manner. We build trust by showing concern for others, particularly when they are vulnerable and in need of support. We don't build trust by asking people to trust us. Those who say, "Trust me," are inviting suspicion. We don't build trust by talking about the importance of trust. Instead, focus on the factors that sustain trust and let it evolve on its own. Trust works most effectively when it is simply part of the way an organization goes about its business. In this respect, trust is best approached indirectly and through actions rather than words.

Trust Presents a Set of Dilemmas to Be Managed

People will sometimes ask, "How do I overcome the distrust that exists within my team?" or "How do I eliminate the distrust that exists between my team and another?" These are appropriate questions as long as one realizes the solution is never final. In asking these questions, many people assume that distrust is a problem that can be solved. In particular, they assume that the appropriate set of words and actions will produce the trust needed within the organization or team. But trust presents us with a series of dilemmas that cannot be easily resolved. For example, how can we demonstrate real concern while eliminating people in an effort to become more cost competitive? Trust requires our demonstrating concern for those with whom we work *and* making the cold-hearted decisions that are sometimes necessary. These are dilemmas that confront us every day as the business environment changes. Trust is not a problem to be solved. It is a dilemma that requires constant attention and an understanding of the tradeoffs inherent in any course of action.

Trust Ultimately Rests on the Character of Our Leaders

Trust is often found in firms whose leaders understand its importance. Founders are particularly important in establishing a culture of trust. At Hewlett-Packard and Motorola, the founders' values permeated the organizational culture. Bill Hewlett, David Packard, and Robert Galvin (who took over Motorola from his father) created companies that reflected their beliefs. On a personal level, they believed in the need to give their employees a great deal of autonomy and trust that they would deliver. In turn, they held themselves to the highest leadership standards so that they would be worthy of the trust placed in them.

Leadership, of course, extends beyond the founders of our largest firms. Consider the team leader who needs to pull together a diverse group of people and work with them to deliver on an aggressive set of performance objectives. The character of the team's leader sets the tone for the group's evolution. Can he or she act in a way that wins the trust of team members? Can he or she trust the team enough to allow members to deliver the results expected of them?

Trusting and trustworthy. Each leader must lead the way in trusting others and behaving in a trustworthy manner. Each leader must take risks along the way and demonstrate, at a personal level, what trust looks like in action. This, ultimately, is the challenge for each of us. Can we learn to trust others in a way that enables them to contribute to the full extent of their talent and drive? To do so, we become more vulnerable, for we begin to depend on others. Can we act in a way that despite pressures to do otherwise, leaves no doubt as to our trustworthiness? When we do so, when we raise the bar in terms of what we expect of ourselves, we open ourselves to failure. Trust, ultimately, requires leaders who are prepared to go first. Then, we must set about building organizations and teams that do the same.

Organization
Assessment Summary

Trust Assessment Summary Sheet

Rating Your Organization or Team

In this organization (or team), people . . .

Exhibit Trust: (from page 37)	Score: _____

✚

Achieve Results: (from page 59)	Score: _____

✚

Act with Integrity: (from page 80)	Score: _____

✚

Demonstrate Concern: (from page 100)	Score: _____

⬇

Sum of All Trust Scores:	Total Score: _____

Trust Summary Rating

Low trust:	Total scores from 32–74
Moderate trust:	Total scores from 75–117
High trust:	Total scores from 118–160

Leadership
Assessment Survey

Use the surveys presented here to assess the degree to which you act in a way that builds trust.

The questions in the first survey assess the degree to which you as a leader, achieve results, act with integrity, and demonstrate concern. They are designed to provoke your thinking regarding the impact of your own behavior as a leader of an organization, group, or team.

For a more systematic approach and perhaps a more accurate picture of your leadership style, use the second survey to solicit the views of others with whom you work. To ensure that people provide you with candid input regarding your leadership style, have a third party collect and summarize the data. The third party may be an internal human resources staff member or an external survey firm or consultant.

Leadership Assessment: Self-Rating

For each question in this survey, select the response that best reflects how you see your own behavior. Choose from among the following responses, and then total your score within each section.

1 = not at all; 2 = to small extent; 3 = to some extent;
4 = to great extent; 5 = to very great extent

You can transfer your overall rating for each trust imperative to the summary at the end to develop an overall leadership profile.

Achieving Results

As a leader, I . . .

1. Have articulated a clear strategic direction that will enable us to win in the marketplace   _____

2. Help people focus on a few key business priorities and clearly stated goals   _____

3. Gain widespread agreement on necessary and roles and accountabilities   _____

1 = not at all; 2 = to small extent; 3 = to some extent;
4 = to great extent; 5 = to very great extent

4. Create a sense of urgency and a drive to succeed _____

5. Make decisions on tough issues in a timely manner _____

6. Give people the resources and autonomy they need in order to be successful _____

7. Invest in and personally support the development and education of others _____

8. Hold people accountable to the highest standards of performance _____

9. Recognize and reward those who are successful and take action (feedback, development, or removal) on those who are not _____

10. Overall, deliver the results I promise _____

Results Total _____

Low Leadership Results	Total = 10 to 22
Moderate Leadership Results	Total = 23 to 37
High Leadership Results	Total = 38 to 50

Acting with Integrity

As a leader, I . . .

11. Am committed to a well-known strategic vision and set of values _____

12. Hold people in the organization to the highest ethical standards _____

13. Openly share my point of view with people at all levels (even when it is at odds with others' beliefs and values) _____

14. Act in a manner that is consistent with my expressed values and beliefs _____

1 = not at all; 2 = to small extent; 3 = to some extent;
4 = to great extent; 5 = to very great extent

15. Deal with reality as it exists, facing the "hard truths" about our business, our products, and our people _____

16. Create an environment where people can, without fear of reprisal, deal with issues in an open and honest manner _____

17. Reveal my true motivations and avoid any form of manipulation in my interactions with others _____

18. Deal fairly with people when problems or issues arise _____

19. "Walk the talk" in following through on my commitments to others _____

20. Overall, act with the highest integrity _____

Integrity Total _____

Low Integrity	Total = 10 to 22
Moderate Integrity	Total = 23 to 37
High Integrity	Total = 38 to 50

Demonstrating Concern

As a leader, I . . .

21. Work to create a common vision and a shared sense of purpose _____

22. Believe that all people are capable of great accomplishments and empower them to act _____

23. Seek to understand the point of view of others and the challenges they face _____

24. Strive to provide the support (training, job opportunities, advice, and so on) that people need to be successful _____

25. Remain accessible to people and willing to engage in mutual dialogue around key business issues _____

1 = not at all; 2 = to small extent; 3 = to some extent;
4 = to great extent; 5 = to very great extent

26. Treat others as partners in the business, sharing both the risks and rewards of performance _____

27. Care about people and treat them as more than a "means to an end" _____

28. Expect people to get results in a way that is consistent with our values _____

29. Give people the flexibility they need to balance the competing demands they face _____

30. Overall, demonstrate concern for people at all levels _____

Concern Total _____

Low Concern	Total = 10 to 22
Moderate Concern	Total = 23 to 37
High Concern	Total = 38 to 50

Overall Rating: Leadership Trustworthiness

Leadership Results Total (from above):_____

Leadership Integrity Total (from above):_____

Leadership Concern Total (from above):_____

Overall Score _____

Low-Trust Leadership	Overall Total = 30 to 69
Moderate-Trust Leadership	Overall Total = 70 to 110
High-Trust Leadership	Overall Total = 111 to 150

1 = not at all; 2 = to small extent; 3 = to some extent;
4 = to great extent; 5 = to very great extent

Leadership Assessment

This survey assesses the leadership style of *[insert name of leader seeking feedback]*. The questions are based on factors that promote organizational and team effectiveness. For each question, select one of the following responses depending on how you see this person operating on a day-to-day basis.

> 1 = not at all; 2 = to small extent; 3 = to some extent;
> 4 = to great extent; 5 = to very great extent

Your responses will be summarized with those of others to ensure confidentiality.

[Provide further detail on where participant should send the survey, deadline for submission, and how input will be used.]

Achieves Results

[insert name of leader asking for input] . . .

1. Has articulated a clear strategic direction that will enable us to win in the marketplace   _____

2. Helps people focus on a few key business priorities and clearly stated goals   _____

3. Gains widespread agreement on necessary actions and accountabilities   _____

4. Creates a sense of urgency and a drive to succeed   _____

5. Makes decisions on tough issues in a timely manner   _____

6. Gives people the resources and autonomy they need in order to be successful   _____

7. Invests in and personally supports the development and education of others   _____

8. Holds people accountable to the highest standards of performance   _____

9. Recognizes and rewards those who are successful and takes action (feedback, development, or removal) on those who are not   _____

10. Overall, delivers the results he or she promises   _____

1 = not at all; 2 = to small extent; 3 = to some extent;
4 = to great extent; 5 = to very great extent

Acts with Integrity

[insert name of leader asking for input] . . .

11. Is committed to a well-known strategic vision and set of values   _____

12. Holds people in the organization to the highest ethical standards   _____

13. Openly shares his or her point of view with people at all levels (even when it is at odds with others' beliefs and values)   _____

14. Acts in a manner that is consistent with his or her expressed values and beliefs   _____

15. Deals with reality as it exists, facing the "hard truths" about our business, our products, and our people   _____

16. Creates an environment where people can deal with issues in an open and honest manner without fear of reprisal   _____

17. Reveals his or her true motivations to others and avoids any form of manipulation in interactions with others   _____

18. Deals fairly with people when problems or issues arise   _____

19. "Walks the talk" in following through on his or her commitments to others   _____

20. Overall, acts with the highest integrity   _____

1 = not at all; 2 = to small extent; 3 = to some extent;
4 = to great extent; 5 = to very great extent

Demonstrates Concern

[insert name of leader asking for input] . . .

21. Works to create a common vision and a shared
    sense of purpose   _____

22. Believes that all people are capable of great
    accomplishments and empowers them to act   _____

23. Seeks to understand the point of view of others
    and the challenges they face   _____

24. Strives to provide the support (training, job
    opportunities, advice, and so on) that people need
    to be successful   _____

25. Remains accessible to people and willing to engage
    in mutual dialogue around key business issues   _____

26. Treats others as partners in the business, sharing
    both the risks and rewards of performance   _____

27. Cares about people and treats them as more than
    a "means to an end"   _____

28. Expects people to get results in a manner consistent
    with our values   _____

29. Strives to give people the flexibility they need to
    balance the competing demands they face   _____

30. Overall, demonstrates concern for people at
    all levels   _____

Thank you for your help in completing this survey. Please send
your response to *[identify third party compiling results]* by *[deadline]*.

1 = not at all; 2 = to small extent; 3 = to some extent;
4 = to great extent; 5 = to very great extent

Notes

Preface

1. R. Shaw, "Trust and Distrust in Organizations: An Intergroup Perspective." Unpublished doctoral dissertation, Yale University, 1989.
2. R. Mayer, J. Davis, and F. Schoorman, "An Integrative Model of Organizational Trust," *Academy of Management Review 20* (3) (1995): 709–34; M. Kramer and T. Tyler, *Trust in Organizations* (Thousand Oaks, Calif.: Sage, 1996); G. Fairholm, *Leadership and the Culture of Trust* (Westport: Praeger, 1994).
3. C. Handy, "Trust and the Virtual Organization," *Harvard Business Review,* May–June (1995): 40–50.
4. F. Fukuyama, *Trust: The Social Virtues and the Creation of Prosperity* (New York: Free Press, 1995).
5. B. Barber, *The Logic and Limits of Trust* (New Brunswick, NJ: Rutgers University Press, 1983).
6. N. Luhman, *Trust and Power* (New York: Wiley, 1980).

Chapter 1

1. F. Fukuyama, *Trust: The Social Virtues and the Creation of Prosperity* (New York: Free Press, 1995); P. Pascarella, "The High Price of Low Trust," *Industry Week,* 6 Nov. 1995, 32–38.
2. M. Keller, *Rude Awakening: The Rise, Fall, and Struggle for Recovery of General Motors* (New York: Morrow, 1989); Keller, *Collision: GM, Toyota, Volkswagen, and the Race to Own the Twenty-first Century* (New York: Doubleday/Currency, 1993).
3. J. S. Hirsch, "Now Hotel Clerks Provide More Than Keys," *Wall Street Journal,* 5 March 1993, B1.
4. J. Champy, *Reengineering Management* (New York: HarperCollins, 1994); M. Hammer, *Beyond Reengineering* (New York: HarperCollins, 1996).

5. C. Handy, *The Age of Unreason* (Boston: Harvard Business School Press, 1989); Handy, "Balancing Corporate Power: A New Federalists Paper," *Harvard Business Review,* Nov.–Dec. (1992): 59–72.

6. F. Fukuyama, *Trust,* 27.

7. "Holding the Hand That Feeds," *The Economist,* 9 Sept. 1995, 65.

8. "Making Strategic Alliances Succeed: The Importance of Trust," *Harvard Business Review,* July–Aug. (1996): 8; T. Ehrenfeld, "Face to Face: Michael Braun," *Inc.,* Aug. (1996): 56–58.

9. M. Yoshino and U. Rangan, *Strategic Alliances* (Boston: Harvard Business School Press, 1995), 123.

10. "Making Strategic Alliances Succeed," 8.

11. Frank Starmer, quoted in J. Lipnack and J. Stamps, *The Age of the Network* (Essex Junction, Vt.: Omneo, 1994).

12. J. Rawnsley, *Total Risk: Nick Leeson and the Fall of Barings Bank* (New York: Harper Business, 1995).

13. Rawnsley, *Total Risk.*

Chapter 2

1. N. Deogun, "A Tough Bank Boss Takes on Computers with Real Trepidation," *Wall Street Journal,* 25 July 1996, A1.

2. R. Mayer, J. Davis, and F. Schoorman, "An Integrative Model of Organizational Trust," *Academy of Management Review 20* (3) (1995): 709–34.

3. N. Luhman, *Trust and Power* (New York: Wiley, 1980), 4.

4. R. Kramer and T. Tyler, *Trust in Organizations: Frontiers of Theory and Research* (Thousand Oaks, Calif.: Sage, 1996); Mayer, Davis, and Schoorman, "An Integrative Model of Organizational Trust," 709–34.

5. J. M. Kouzes and B. Z. Posner, *Credibility: How Leaders Gain and Lose It, Why People Demand It* (San Francisco: Jossey-Bass, 1993).

Chapter 3

1. "Cancer Patient Dies in Chicago After Chemotherapy Overdose," *New York Times,* 18 June 1995, A17.

2. G. McWilliams, "Desperate Hours at DEC," *Business Week,* 9 May 1994, 26–29.

3. P. Judge, "Digital's PC Pratfall," *Business Week,* 15 July 1996, 28.

4. W. Calloway, in "Who We Are . . . Where We Are Going," PepsiCo publication, no date.

5. D. Wechsler and B. Upbin, "Hewlett-Packard: Performer of the Year," *Forbes,* 1 Jan. 1996, 67.

6. D. Packard, "The End of an Era," *Measure* (Hewlett-Packard publication), Nov.–Dec. (1993): 4.

7. *Corporate Objectives,* Hewlett-Packard publication, no date.

8. J. Welch, "GE: Just Your Average Everyday $60 Billion Family Grocery Store," *Industry Week,* 2 May 1994, 13–18.

9. W. Steer, "Key Leadership Challenges for Present and Future Executives." In F. Hesselbein, M. Goldsmith, and R. Beckhard (eds.), *The Leader of the Future* (San Francisco: Jossey-Bass, 1995), 266–67.

10. Fukuyama, *Trust,* 155.

11. C. Weatherup, "Tough Trust," *Leader to Leader, 3* (Winter 1997): 46–54; interview with D. Hatch, April 1996, Armonk, N.Y.

12. B. Hewlett, "The Human Side of Management." Clark Executive lecture at University of Notre Dame, 25 March 1982.

13. D. Dammerman, speech given to National Association of Black Accountants, St. Louis, Mo., 28 June 1991.

14. AlliedSignal 1995 Annual Report; N. Tichy and R. Charan, "The CEO as Coach: An Interview with AlliedSignal's Lawrence A. Bossidy," *Harvard Business Review,* March–April (1995): 69–78.

15. "CEO of the Year: Larry Bossidy of AlliedSignal," *Financial World,* 29 March 1994, 44–52.

16. Lawrence A. Bossidy, speech presented to Corning Business Leaders Roundtable Forum, Corning, N.Y., 24 June 1996.

17. Tichy and Charan, "The CEO as Coach," 69–78.

Chapter 4

1. J. Badaracco and R. Ellsworth, *Leadership and the Quest for Integrity* (Boston: Harvard Business School Press, 1989), 99.

2. GE 1991 Annual Report, 5.

3. "Trust in Me," *The Economist,* 16 Dec. 1995, 16.

4. A. Myerson, "Follow the Leader: In a Company Move, the Mountain May Come to the Chief," *New York Times,* 13 Oct. 1995, D1.

5. "Cross Currents" section in *At Work: Stories of Tomorrow's Workplace 3* (3) (May–June 1994) (San Francisco: Berrett-Koehler): 16.

6. C. Weatherup, "Tough Trust," *Leader to Leader, 3* (Winter 1997): 46–54.

7. R. Calvin, "Corporate Social Responsibility Is Not a Challenge." Chapter 14 in J. Houck and O. Williams, eds., *Is the Good Corporation Dead? Social Responsibility in a Global Economy* (Lanham, Md.: Rowman & Littlefield, 1996), 253–66.

8. R. Henkoff, "Keeping Motorola on a Roll," *Fortune,* 18 April 1994, 67.

9. J. McKenna, "Bob Galvin Predicts Life After Perfection," *Industry Week,* 21 Jan. 1991, 12–15.

Chapter 5

1. D. Packard, *The HP Way* (New York: Harper Business, 1995), 129–30.
2. Packard, *The HP Way,* 132.
3. In *At Work: Stories of Tomorrow's Workplace 4* (2) (March–April 1995) (San Francisco: Berrett-Koehler): 3.
4. *The HP Way,* Hewlett-Packard publication, 1989.
5. *The Test of Time,* Hewlett-Packard publication, no date; M. Beer and C. Rogers, *Human Resources at Hewlett-Packard (Case A),* Harvard Business School case no. 9–495–051, 1995.
6. A. Sloan, "The Hit Men," *Newsweek,* 26 Feb. 1996, 44–48.
7. Interview with S. Kerr, April 1996, Crotonville, NY.
8. C. Whiting and C. Popper, *Managing for Commitment: Using Work-Life Initiatives to Build Employee Commitment and Deliver Business Results.* DuPont Case Study presented at the Human Resource Planning Society National Conference, Palm Springs, Calif., March 1996.
9. M. Galen, "Work and Family," *Business Week,* 28 June 1993, 80–88.
10. Fukuyama, *Trust,* 358.
11. Packard, *The HP Way,* 127.
12. S. McCartney, "Management: Airline Industries' Top-Ranked Woman Keeps Southwest's Small-Fry Spirit Alive," *Wall Street Journal,* 30 Nov. 1995, B1.
13. "Giving It Away," *The Economist,* 23 April 1994, 67.
14. "Employee Ownership Report," *Companies,* Nov.-Dec. (1995): 10.
15. D. Anfuso, "PepsiCo Shares Power and Wealth with Workers," *Personnel Journal 47* (6) (June 1995): 49.
16. Packard, *The HP Way,* 136–37.
17. Packard, *The HP Way,* 128–29.

Chapter 6

1. Interview with T. Kaney, June 1996, Philadelpha, PA; W. Bennis and B. Nanus, *Leaders: The Strategies for Taking Charge* (New York: Harper-Collins, 1985), 153.
2. As part of their studies on credibility and leadership in the early 1980s and 1990s, Kouzes and Posner asked people from a variety of firms and levels what "they most look for and admire in a leader, someone whose direction they would *willingly* follow." J. Kouzes and B. Posner, *The Leadership Challenge* (San Francisco: Jossey-Bass, 1995), 20.

3. D. Henriques, "Preaching But Not Practicing?," *New York Times*, 22 Dec. 1995, D1.
4. R. Hudson, "Feuding Executives Lose Their Jobs at Cable and Wireless," *Wall Street Journal*, 22 Nov. 1995, A4.
5. Lee Iacocca, *Iacocca* (New York: Bantam Books, 1984), 145.
6. C. Bartlett, *3M: Profile of an Innovating Company*, Harvard Business School case no. 9–395016 (3 Jan. 1995): 15.

Chapter 7

1. R. Farson, *Management of the Absurd* (New York: Simon & Schuster, 1996), 131.
2. J. Welch, "Turning Soft Values into Hard Results," *Leaders Magazine* *16* (4) (Oct.–Nov.–Dec. 1993): 38–40.
3. Fukuyama, *Trust*, 224.
4. C. Argyris, *Overcoming Organizational Defenses* (Needham Heights, Mass.: Allyn & Bacon, 1990).
5. J. Weber, "A Big Company That Works," *Business Week*, 4 May 1992, 126.
6. M.F.R. Kets de Vries, "Making a Giant Dance," *Across the Board*, Oct. (1994): 27–32.
7. C. Taylor-Bodmer, "More Than Just Hands," *Hemispheres*, 2 March 1995, 13.
8. Packard, *The HP Way*, 141.
9. Packard, *The HP Way*, 72.
10. R. Half, "Hewlett-Packard Digs Deep for Digital Future," *Business Week*, 18 Oct. 1993, 72–75.
11. W. Zellner, "Go-Go Goliaths," *Business Week*, 13 Feb. 1995, 64–70.
12. C. Bermant, "For the Latest in Corporate Training, Try a CD-ROM," *New York Times*, 16 Oct. 1995, C5.
13. "Company Throws the Books at Workers to Boost Learning, Earning, and Growth," *Lakewood Report*, June (1995): 8.
14. B. Moskal, "Hide This Report Card," *Industry Week*, 19 Sept. 1994, 28.
15. "In the News" section in *At Work: Stories of Tomorrow's Workplace 4* (2) (March–April 1995) (San Francisco: Berrett-Koehler): 5.
16. J. Fierman, "Winning Ideas from Maverick Managers," *Fortune*, 6 Feb. 1996, 68.
17. Packard, *The HP Way*, 159.
18. G. Hill and K. Hamada, "Motorola Illustrates How an Aged Giant Can Remain Vibrant," *Wall Street Journal*, 9 Dec. 1992, A1.
19. "Cat Fights and Straw Men," *Fast Company* (premiere issue, 1995): 152.

Chapter 8

1. J. Welch, "Soft Values for a Hard Decade: A View on Winning in the '90s." Executive speech reprint, Corporate Publications, GE Company, Nov. 1989.
2. B. Morris, "The Wealth Builders," *Fortune*, 11 Dec. 1995, 96.
3. Morris, "The Wealth Builders," 99.
4. Fukuyama, *Trust*, 153.
5. C. Weatherup, "Tough Trust," *Leader to Leader*, 3 (Winter 1997): 46–54.
6. J. Welch, "Turning Soft Values into Hard Results," 38–40.
7. C. Handy, *Age of Paradox* (Boston: Harvard University Press, 1994).
8. M. Maremont, "Kodak's New Focus," *Business Week*, 30 Jan. 1995, 62–68.
9. Packard, *The HP Way*, 157.
10. T. Stewart, "Managing in a Wired Company," *Fortune*, 11 July 1994, 56.
11. A. Markels, "A Power Producer Is Intent on Giving Power to Its People," *Wall Street Journal*, 3 Jul. 1995, A1.
12. Bartlett, "3M: Profile of an Innovative Company," 5.
13. Packard, *The HP Way*, 135–36.

Chapter 9

1. Fukuyama, *Trust*, 362.
2. R. Farson, *Management of the Absurd*, 43.
3. Morris, "The Wealth Builders," 88.
4. R. Pascale, *Managing on the Edge: How the Smartest Companies Use Conflict to Stay Ahead* (New York: Simon & Schuster, 1990), 244.
5. GE Annual Report, 1991, 5.
6. J. Welch, "Competitiveness and Integrity." Executive speech reprint, Corporate Publications, GE Company, July 1992, 3.
7. M. Maremont and J. Barnathan, "Blind Ambition: How the Pursuit of Results Got Out of Hand for B&L," *Business Week*, 23 Oct. 1995, 78–92.
8. Maremont and Barnathan, "Blind Ambition," 78–92.
9. N. Kleinfield, "The Company as One Happy Family: No More," *New York Times*, 4 March 1996, A1.
10. J. Keller, "AT&T's Robert Allen Gets Sharp Criticism Over Layoffs, Losses," *Wall Street Journal*, 22 Feb. 1996, A1.
11. J. Keller, "AT&T Is Offering Buyout Packages to About One-half of Its Supervisory Force," *Wall Street Journal*, 15 Nov. 1995, A3.
12. New York Times, *The Downsizing of America* (New York: Times Books, 1996), 51–53.

13. New York Times, *The Downsizing of America*, 51–53.
14. R. Tomasko, *Downsizing: Reshaping the Corporation for the Future* (New York: AMACOM, 1990); M. Moravec and R. Knowdell, *From Downsizing to Recovery: Strategic Transition Options for Organizations and Individuals* (Palo Alto, Calif.: CPP Books, 1994).
15. "OAW Guide Is a Profile of High-Performance Companies," *Work in America*, Sept. (1994): 3–5.
16. "Cross Currents" section in *At Work: Stories of Tomorrow's Workplace 3* (3) (May–June 1994) (San Francisco: Berrett-Koehler): 16.
17. Interview with L. Evans of Right Associates, May 1996, Philadelphia, PA.
18. S. Baker, "And Now, Designer Oil?" *Business Week*, 19 Sept. 1994, 58.

Chapter 10

1. J. Nordheimer, "Borman Plans to Stay for Now," *New York Times*, 26 Feb. 1986, D1.
2. Nordheimer, "Borman Plans to Stay," D1.
3. Galbraith, *Designing Organizations* (San Francisco: Jossey-Bass, 1996).
4. "Employee Motivation," *Incentive*, May (1992): 31–34.
5. Nordstrom Employee Handbook.
6. S. McCartney, "Piloted by Bethune, Continental Air Lifts Its Workers' Morale," *Wall Street Journal*, 15 May 1996, A1; W. Zellner, "The Right Place, the Right Time," *Business Week*, 27 May 1996, 74.
7. Telephone interview with G. Brenneman of Continental, August 1996, Houston, TX.

Chapter 11

1. Fukuyama, *Trust*, 31–32.
2. Packard, *The HP Way*.
3. HP 1995 Employee Survey, provided December 1996 by Peter Ulrich.
4. Fukuyama, *Trust*.
5. New York Times, *The Downsizing of America*.
6. Fukuyama, *Trust*, 342.

Index